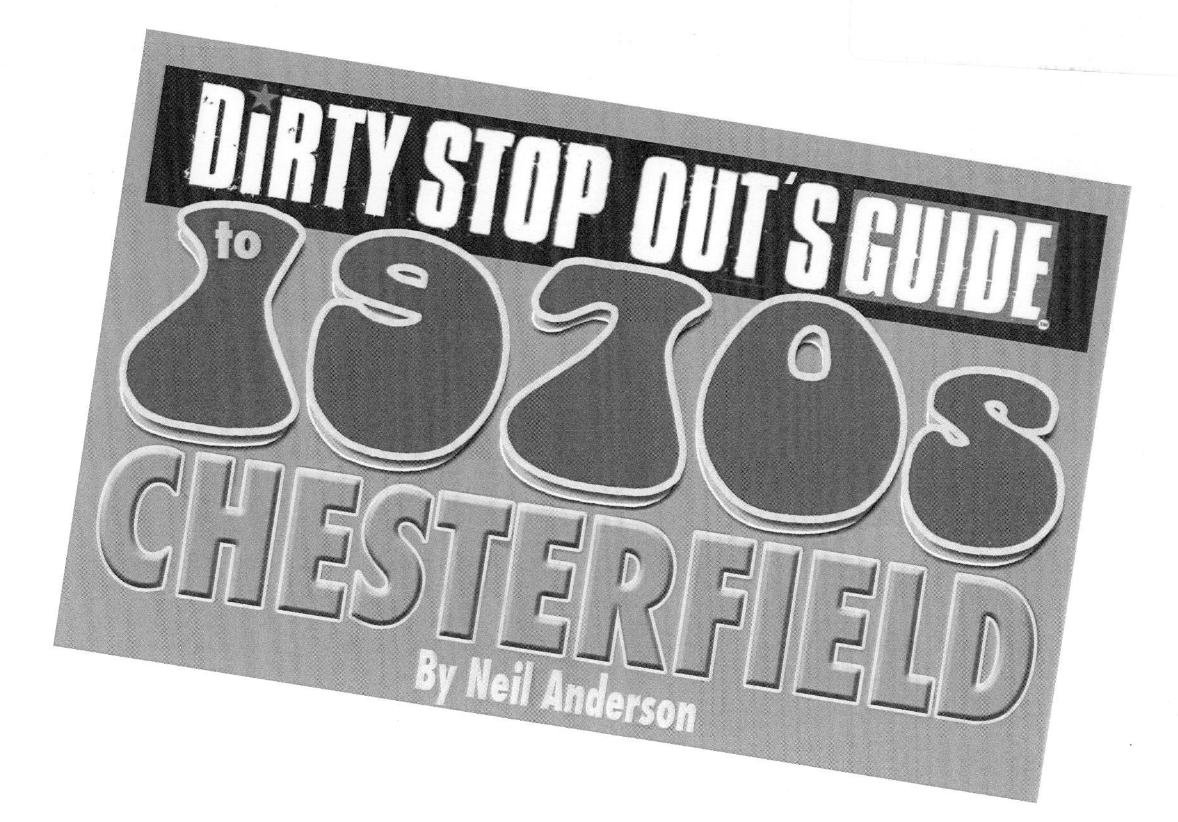

The all-conquering Aquarius

ISBN 978-1-908431-28-8

Every effort has been made to trace the copyright holders of photographers
in this book but one or two were unreachable. We would be grateful if the
photographers concerned would contact us.

The opinions expressed by contributors to this publication are not necessarily
the opinions of ACM Retro Ltd or Neil Anderson. ACM Retro Ltd and Neil Anderson
assumes no responsibility for such content.

Published by ACM Retro Ltd

Registered office :

51 Clarkegrove Road
Sheffield
S10 2NH

Visit ACM Retro at: www.acmretro.com

A catalogue record for this book is available from the British Library.

Vinyl outlets were in abundance in the era

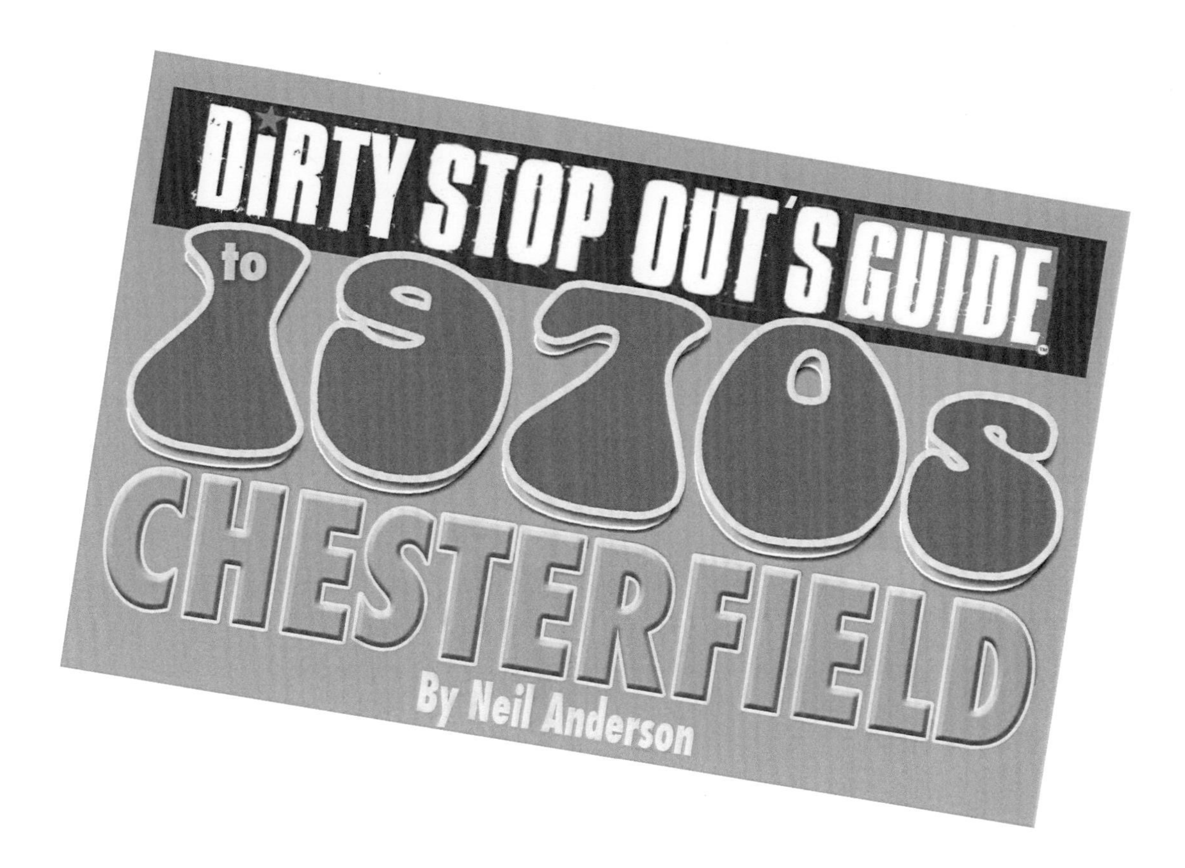

Derby Road safety campaigners

Roxy Bowie

FUSION
DISCOTHEQUE

Visage
Kraftwerk
Human League
Joy Division

Ultravox
John Foxx
Spandall Ballet
Orch. Manoeuvres

FUSION GOES
FUTURIST
Every Thursday night
D.J. JIMMY MACK
plays the new romantic & electro music
THURSDAY 26th MARCH
"MUSIC FOR PLEASURE"
Live on Stage
plus
"THE EXPELAIRES"
Admission only 50p each with this Ticket
Valid for 1 or 2 persons
THURSDAYS — FUSION GOES FUTURIST
9.00 p.m. to 2.00 a.m. Over 18's
The Management reserves the right
to refuse admission
Hollywell Street, Chesterfield 32694

"I really don't think you could have found a better town to grow up in than Chesterfield in the 1970s. The sounds, the fashions, the venues - the variety was amazing. I really wouldn't have swapped it for any other decade", Mark Sanderson.

CONTENTS

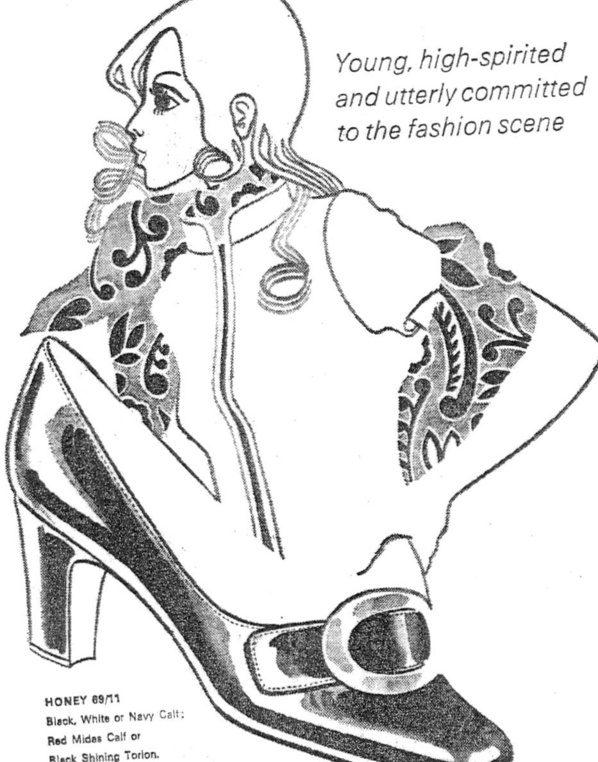

HONEY 69/11
Black, White or Navy Calf;
Red Midas Calf or
Black Shining Torlon.
2" heel.

32, FARGATE, SHEFFIELD. 1/3, STEPHENSON PLACE, CHESTERFIELD

J.B Whites - these days better known as Strand Cards

Dave Stone (right) and his dad Bas Stone, a man that got more than a few locals through their test in the era via his Bas Stone Driving School

Popular 1970s event the Chesterfield Carnival is all set for a relaunch in July 2014 to raise money for Ashgate Hospice

Courtesy of Chesterfield Photographic Society and www.picturethepast.org.uk

Looking towards the Market Hall

Charity drinking matches were all the rage in seventies Chesterfield

Looking over the 'donut' car park

FORGET THE STEREOTYPES - LIFE IN SEVENTIES CHESTERFIELD ROCKED!

If there was ever a decade with an image problem it was the 1970s.

Line it up alongside its post-war counterparts and it looks like a total car crash of an era comprising nothing more than strikes, jaw-droppingly bad fashion and general social unrest.

The fifties, like every other decade bar the 1970s, seems only ever viewed through rose-tinted spectacles.

It's commonly referred to as a 'golden age' of innovation, rock'n'roll and the decade that saw the rise of the television and labour saving devices, like the washing machine, as the country slowly eased its way out of post-war austerity.

The 'swinging' sixties are defined by the dominance of the Beatles, fashions like the mini-skirt, flower power and free love, whilst the 1980s are all about big hair, bigger shoulder pads and brick-like mobile phones.

No such luck for the seventies; power cuts, three-day-weeks, racial tension, football hooligans, sectarian violence, mad hair and flared trousers are normally the images conjured up by the media.

There's no doubt the stereotypes existed, but look beyond them and you'll not find it hard to find gushingly affectionate memories of the era taste apparently forgot.

In fact, to those in their formative years - i.e. those who were more concerned with partying and their Thursday night fill of Top of the Pops - the era was the stuff of dreams.

Fashions went full circle, from Oxford bags to skin tight drainpipes; music went from bloated rock to three chord punk, with glam and disco taking up the rear and everything from

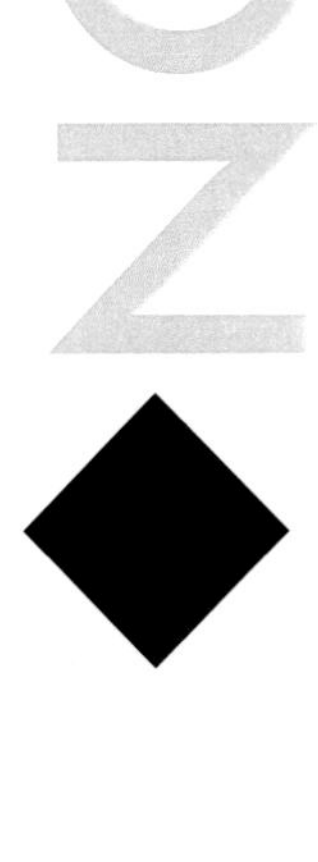

the Clangers to the Wombles filled the shiny new colour TVs.

The scorching hot summer of '76 is still talked about; Chesterfield hit it head on with a frothing pint of Mansfield lager in one hand and a Frederick's ice cream in the other.

The seventies was the era of cabaret and nowhere did it better than the town's Aquarius - a true magnet for revellers from right around the region.

So many things demonstrate just how different thinking was in the era; soft porn visited the cinemas; strip shows were more commonplace than Starbucks are today; racism was accepted light entertainment and drinking competitions got you a pat on the back from your local charity, rather than a flea in the ear from your local health spokesperson.

All in all there was more than enough to forget the politically-charged atmosphere of the era including Bloody Sunday, Margaret Thatcher taking charge of the Conservative Party, the 'Winter of Discontent' and the high profile assassinations of Lord Mountbatten and Norris McWhirter.

There's no doubt that the beginning of the seventies in Chesterfield was an affluent and confident time as the sun was setting on the hippy revolution of the late 1960s.

The era brought luxuries and new experiences the older generations could have barely imagined.

There was the massive boom in package tour holidays abroad - something unthinkable just a few years earlier

Few bands gave the youth (well mostly the female section) a style makeover quite like the arrival of the Bay City Rollers and even a liberal lashing of Brut aftershave couldn't disguise the familiar stench of an Afghan coat.

Elvis died but John Travolta and Grease signalled a rebirth for rock'n'roll.

Viva 1970s Chesterfield - it truly rocked!

Bread queues grow longer

JUST SEVEN DAYS after returning to work, disillusioned about the effects of their unofficial stoppage, bakery workers at a major Chesterfield plant struck again at 6 a.m. on Tuesday — and this time it was official.

SINCE the walk-out at the Mother's Pride bakery at Upper Newbold — in line with the national call by the Bakery Workers' Union — the bread queues have daily grown longer.

"Britain's bakers are seeking a brand new wage agreement which would give them £40 for a 40-hour week — so far they have been offered £30 a week.

The decision to call for a national stoppage — almost unheard of in the industry — came at the week-end following the breakdown of national pay talks.

It appears that unless there are dramatic new moves the strike could still be with us in the middle of next week.

The 130 workers at Mother's Pride walked off the job at 6 a.m. on Tuesday, and since then no bread has been baked. During their unofficial stoppage, supervisory staff at the bakery kept supplies going for a few days, but this has not happened this time.

Stockpiling

Local public reaction has been predictable. As soon as the strike was announced, housewives began stockpiling.

Since Tuesday, bakeries owned by "independents" have had to face early-morning queues — queues which in some cases have lasted well into the afternoon as bakeries tried to meet the demand.

As well as buying mass-produced bread, housewives have started to bake their own.

Mr. Charles Dauncey, director of Thomas Irv[illegible] and Co. Ltd., corn merchants of Chesterfield, said yes[illegible] day that they were selling [illegible] much flour and yeast [illegible] day as they were selling a week before the stri[illegible]

Outside their shop on [illegible] Beetwell Street, queues [illegible] stretched more than 50 y[illegible]

At present they are [illegible] six tons of flour a day [illegible] about seven - hundredw[illegible] of yeast. So far there [illegible] been no word of ratio[illegible]

The problem could [illegible] the strike drags, [illegible] bakery flying squad [illegible] flour mills and yeas[illegible]

Field d[illegible]

The independe[illegible] have had a fiel[illegible] the strike — b[illegible] already saying [illegible] be glad to get b[illegible] business.

A spokesma[illegible] Parker and [illegible] worth Road, [illegible] were baking [illegible] much bread [illegible] this was af[illegible] duction of [illegible]

To boost [illegible] had start[illegible] bread bak[illegible]

But he [illegible] are conc[illegible] very gl[illegible] over to[illegible]

"I've got a loaf . . ." Mrs. Jessie Cooper (70), of Hill Top Road, New Whittington, reckoned that her wait from 7.30 a.m. to nine a.m. at Davy's, Packers Row, Chesterfield on Tuesday was well worth while — she was first in the queue.

THE AGE OF AQUARIUS

Enjoying a night at the Aquarius

Chesterfield really had seen nothing like the Aquarius when it opened in 1972.

Only a chicken in a basket meal stood between you and some of the biggest names in entertainment.

Cabaret was sweeping the country and the people of the town decided they wanted a slice of the Las Vegas glitz in the shadow of the Crooked Spire.

Though the town's Working Men's Clubs offered entertainment and bingo aplenty, they could never compete with the palatial Aquarius.

Nobody was in the thick of the action more than early Aquarius compere and all round showman, Chesterfield's own Bernie Clifton.

His career was on vertical trajectory in the seventies and much of it was played out at the venue.

He said: "In 1973 I was already doing quite well on the cabaret circuit and I used to compere at Batley Variety Club and I used to sing a lot. But then something happened to my voice and I turned into a monotone. It was something to do with the nodules on my vocal chords and I had to stop work. It happened at a time that Eddie Buchanan, who had been compere at the Aquarius, had decided to leave. It was like fate as I just fell into the job and I only lived 100 yards away from the stage door. I used to leave my house, walk through the neighbour's garden and I was in the Aquarius car park.

"I ended up having to rest my voice for three months and I worked at the Aquarius through the summer of 1973. But as a result of that, John Williamson the Aquarius owner, offered me the job of booking the acts. I used to work above the Blue Bell pub which used to be

Punchbowl Entertainments. I was in the office all day on the phone to the London agents. I'd then go home, have my tea and it would then be down to the Aquarius. I did that for about nine months.

"I remember booking Cannon and Ball, it was £300. They turned up for the band call on the Sunday afternoon and were horrified to find they were topping the bill. They were quaking in their boots and they said they'd never topped a bill before. They said, 'We're a support act'. We took a chance because we knew how popular they were. They ended up topping the bill and went down a storm."

It's fair to say the duo never looked back after that.

"The Aquarius was so good for me as they used to get the same people in various nights of the week, so I could never do the same act twice. I had to constantly come up with pranks and japes and new ideas.

"The Sunday night crowd was always best.

"In the summer of '73 I'd still got a few bookings in other places to honour. One was for a police club in Leeds and it was quite well paid so I needed a night off, so I rang Marti Caine up and she agreed to cover me at the Aquarius."

Bernie agreed to leave a cheque for the £10 payment behind the reception desk for her.

"I went to Leeds, did the show and when I returned on Thursday I said to Margaret that worked on reception, 'Did Marti pick the cheque up?'. She said, 'Yes'.

"In 1975 I'm in Wales doing a tour of the clubs with my voice back and by this time Marti had won New Faces and her career was in orbit. She was top of the bill at the Stoneleigh Club in Porthcawl so I decided to go backstage and congratulate her on her success.

"She said, 'I've been waiting for you - sit down'. So I sat down and she went through her handbag and said, 'I've been carrying this round for two years'. It was her cheque. I looked at her and said, 'Why haven't you cashed it?' She said, 'Look at the bloody date' and I realised I'd missed the date by a year and in those days if you didn't cash a cheque within three months it was gone.

"She said, 'You wouldn't believe how much I needed that tenner!' and I said, 'I swear it was a complete accident'.

"I always remember Bernard Manning coming. It was a Rotary Club function which would quite often happen on a Monday or a Tuesday. They'd booked it months in advance without knowing the line-up. They all turned up dressed for dinner and I always remember the head Rotarian coming backstage asking if he could have a word with Mr Manning. And I said, 'Yes, no problem'.

"Bernard said, 'Alright squire' and the Rotarian said, 'I hope you don't mind me mentioning this but we have our ladies with us this evening and we would be so grateful if you would tone your act to suit the company that's out there'. And Bernard said, 'Don't worry pal, done a lot of these. It'll be fine'.

"Well to say that to Bernard was like a red rag to a bull. He went out and his first gag went along the lines of , '...Well he's giving her one, and he's giving her one good. And then she said, 'Just a minute, before you carry on, don't you think you should take precautions?' And he said, 'I have done, I've tied a plank across mi arse'.

"Within ten minutes he'd emptied the club. He absolutely went for their throats. Talk about the wrong place at the wrong time for the Rotarians.

"The people that did stay that night were in hysterics.

"We had the Dallas Boys who, in the '70s, were a very successful cabaret act. But in the '50s, twenty years earlier, they had been a very successful TV act. Like most things, their time came and went but they were doing well in the clubs.

"Well we were having a good week and there'd been a lot of banter with them and it got to the last night. Well in my loft I'd found a copy of one of their sheet music hits from the

AQUARIUS

The Chairman and the pop star

That amiable but apparently semi-literate official of the Wheeltappers and Shunters Social Club, Chairman Colin Crompton, is the main attraction at the Aquarius Club, Chesterfield, next week, where he will soon alter that plush nightclub atmosphere! On Monday, for one night only the former pop idol Del Shannon, still very much in the pop business though he has been around since 1961, will visit the club. Remember his "Hats off to Larry."

1950s. It was called 'One Finger, One Thumb, Keep Moving'. The picture on the front was of the five guys with their thumbs up.

"I went to their dressing room during the day and did the whole thing up like a shrine thinking 'they'll love this'. I put the photograph up of how they were and put some flowers around it and candles with the words 'Lest We Forget, Where Are They Now'. Not forgetting that was 20 years ago and 20 years is a long time.

"So I waited for their return with relish and they turned up about an hour before they were due on. Well they went absolutely bloody mad. They didn't get it at all. They went absolutely ballistic.

"'Who did this?' they demanded to know. And Stan Dallas, subsequently a very successful agent, was the kind of mediator. One guy - Leon - had a short fuse and he was going to tear whoever had done this limb from limb.

"Well I had to looked shocked and say 'What?' 'That's terrible'.

"I then had to blame it on someone else and said, 'I think I know who it is. It's that bloody waiter who thinks he's a comic'. And they said, 'Which one'. And I said, 'Oh no, he's not on tonight'.

"I got away with my life that night.

"Probably the one aspect of my tenure there that stuck out were the presentations. They started to become a kind of a cult thing. The first half of the evening would be support acts and then a long interval - maybe an hour. And then you'd start the presentations and you'd end up with probably half a dozen hen parties coming in. The prospective bride would be dragged up on stage and then all these obscene items would come out of a box. There'd also be champagne, drinks, flowers and photographs being taken by Gerald the photographer.

"The Aquarius was the place to come and celebrate.

"I always felt sorry for the main acts of the evening because of instead of going on at midnight they would be wondering if these presentations would ever finish.

"Then there was Big George Naufahu, the head of security - he was a man mountain and former boxer. He was about six foot four. He never needed to exert any physical violence as his presence was enough.

"They were great days and it just won't happen again."

New compere for Aquarius

Starting on Sunday "Aquarius" will have a new resident compere, Bernie Clifton, as reported last week.

After several years, Bernie has now established himself as one of the leading comedy entertainers on the Northern Clubland Circuit.

His recent T.V. appearances included a spot on the B.B.C. Television show, "The Good Old Days," and as a result of his success on the show, he took part in the stage version at the Winter Gardens, Blackpool, last summer.

Bernie is no stranger to compering, having just completed a season at the world famous Batley Variety Club with such names as Shirley

Vince returns to Aquarius Club

VINCE HILL stars at the Aquarius Club, Chesterfield, during July 21 week—having recently returned from Knokke in Belgium, where he starred in the B.B.C. entry that won the Golden Seaswallow Festival.

It is also an important week for Vince, because on the day before he opens at Chesterfield his latest record, 'Brother Sun Sister Moon' is released, and on Sunday, July 29 he will be appearing in 'The Golden Shot' singing the new record.

Earlier this year Vince enjoyed great success with his first ever British T.V. series, 'They Sold a Million' on B.B.C.2, and now plans are in hand to repeat six of the best shows on B.B.C.1 in the Autumn, followed by a brand new series in 1974. He will also be seen hosting his own T.V. show shortly, when he will be featured in B.B.C.'s 'My Kind of Music' series.

Vince has an extensive list of cabaret engagements taking him well into 1974.

Happily married and the proud father of a 20-month-old son, Vince now drives a Rolls-Royce and lives in a luxurious house in Hertfordshire, complete with private lake and swimming pool.

Enjoying a night at the 'Acca'

Enjoying a night at the 'Acca'

Facing up to the new season

WHEN Cheesterfield F.C. players reported back for training at Saltergate on Monday, club Chairman Mr. Dan Newton reaffirmed the Board's determination to restore Chesterfield as a Second Division Club.

He recalled that last season hopes were high of success but injuries, followed by inconsistency, disrupted what was considered a well-balanced side.

"We struggled to maintain Third Division status", he continued, "and found ourselves with a loss of £36,000. It must be emphasized that unless players produce the success required on the field, bringing in the spectators, we as a Board cannot stand losses of this nature.

"Today we officially welcome our new manager in whom we have placed our trust in his ambition to become a successful manager", Mr. Newton continued.

Obviously recalling the many times last season when the team took the field in all-white strips, Mr. Newton reminded the players that the club's official colours are blue and white "and these colours must be worn in all home matches and whenever possible away," he said.

In concluding Mr. Newton urged the players to "get the club back into the Second Division where it rightly belongs. Make up your minds to be one of the promotion sides".

Team Manager Joe Shaw, in welcoming the players back, said that hard work lay ahead. "I wish everyone the best of luck," he said, "and I hope this will be a season to remember".

The only new face to report for training was Ken Burton, given a free transfer by Sheffield Wednesday but at Chesterfield on a three months' trial.

Our picture shows the Manager, Mr. Shaw (front left) meeting some of his players. Back row (left to right): Terry Henderson (trialist), Frank Large, Jim Kabia, Sam Ferris, Ray McHale, Arthur Bellamy, Jim Brown; front (left to right): Mr. Shaw, Andy Kowalski, Albert Holmes, Steve Downes and Ken Burton.

The early to mid-1970s were the high point of the cabaret scene in the UK but Chesterfield's Aquarius was more successful than most - it lasted right through the 1980s as well. Here's a selection of some of the favourites from the era.

Next time the fudge.
NORMAN COLLIER
Agent DOROTHY SOLOMON ASSOCIATED ARTISTES LTD.
PICCADILLY HOUSE 33 LOWER REGENT STREET
LONDON SW1Y 4NE
Telephone 01 734 9766
Best Wishes
Jimmy Ruffin
New single "Thank You Girl"
2058 901
New album "Jimmy Ruffin"
2383 240
polydor
MARKETED BY POLYDOR LIMITED

Marti Caine - the Sheffield star that was big hit at the Aquarius

FAINTING AT 'THE EXORCIST'

Queuing at the off licence

The 1970s hailed some truly gargantuan films - many of them still more than capable of packing the cinemas out four decades on.

Some were so influential that they helped define the cultural fabric of the era.

No supernatural film has ever had quite the impact as 'The Exorcist' which was first released in 1973.

The hype surrounding it was huge and the media were awash with reports of audiences fainting and vomiting in the States where it was first aired.

And things weren't much different when Satan's cloven cinematic hoof first trotted onto English soil.

Some councils in the UK were that hysterical they banned it outright. But the British entrepreneurial spirit soon found a way around it. 'Exorcist Bus Trips' started appearing to take moviegoers to neighbouring towns to see it!

Thankfully there was no such problem in Chesterfield. 'The Exorcist', complete with projectile vomiting, spinning head and everything else the devil could throw at it, was shown in all its horrifying glory.

It's fair to say, some people are still getting over it.

Eileen Marriott: "I saw this with a boyfriend at the ABC, it spooked me especially as they announced there were church people you could talk to if you were affected by it. We had to leave half way through as I was totally freaked out. That night alone in bed I couldn't sleep and was convinced the bed was moving! This happened even though I had previously read the book with no effect on me. I would NEVER watch it again ! Give me a nice musical any day!!!"

Linda Jean Stevens: "Must admit I was too scared to go to the cinema to see it at the time

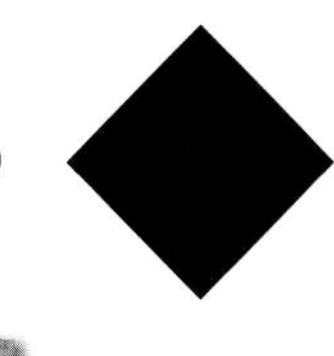

because of all the hype... Have seen it on TV since!! It probably had more of an impact on the big screen, like 'Friday the 13th'."

Paula Drew: "What a film. Still scares me to this day."

Jan Frobisher: "I remember vividly, my R.E teacher, John Pickering trying to stop me from going in. Don't think anyone got persuaded otherwise, but each to their own..."

Lesley McGregor: "I saw this at the ABC between my fingers. Luckily there were some very silly boys there that night who lightened the whole thing. Walking home down the Lido path in Wingerworth was traumatic though."

Les Jones: "Kids at our school were talking about nothing else for weeks!"

Paramedics were on standby all over the States as regular calls rained in of people fainting or simply going into full blown hysterics when the film was first doing the rounds.

The hype around 'The Exorcist' is still unparalleled in supernatural circles - even the furore created by the 'Blair Witch Project' a quarter of century later seems almost pedestrian at the side of it.

Though it didn't spin heads around (in this case it simply bit them off) 'Jaws' rewrote the rulebooks in terms of a hit film.

It became the highest grossing movie ever at the time and boasted one of the most menacing film scores in history (something that apparently only rose to prominence because the mechanical shark kept breaking down and they needed a way of filling gaping holes in the film!) 'Jaws' merchandising - everything from games to shark fins to attach to your back to scare friends at the beach to T-shirts and games - seemed to be absolutely everywhere.

It's fair to say a swim in the sea never had quite the same appeal after a viewing of 'Jaws'.

The film turned the movie world on its head. Never had a summer release done business like this and all was going swimmingly until 'Star Wars'...

The success of that film caught everyone unawares - not least the cast and crew.

Director George Lucas was that convinced it would be a flop he hightailed it off to Hawaii. It wasn't until he caught the teatime CBS news that he realised he was about to become very rich.

Even the model makers were soon signing autographs!

But there were also plenty of people who preferred keeping their feet on the dance floors of Planet Earth rather than outer space.

'Saturday Night Fever' helped popularise disco music like never before and helped signal the demise of the cabaret club and its expensive artists.

It shot John Travolta to worldwide fame and the Bee Gees soundtrack became one of the biggest selling albums of its kind... ever!

He wasn't away from our screens for long. He shot back bigger than ever for the 1978 smash 'Grease' with Olivia Newton-John.

Sally Litton said: "I never seemed to be away from the cinema in the 1970s. There really were so many great films. I still love 'Grease' after all these years. So many great songs!"

Looking towards the Crooked Spire on the approach to the seventies

Football hooliganism was on the rise across Britain in the era and Chesterfield was more than noted for its eagerness to partake

(left) The Queen's Silver Jubilee celebrations could take on many forms

Courtesy of Derbyshire Local Studies Library and www.picturethepast.org.uk

Seventies-style 'selfie' via the humble photo booth

All dressed up in '70s Chesterfield

Cathedral Vaults was better known as 'Pretty Windows'

The long gone Pepperdays

More outspoken fashion

The Ford Cortina - essential transport of the era

Boden's Restaurant in all its glory

WHEN THE LIGHTS WENT OUT

A busy Saturday night

Six million working days were lost to strikes in the first six months of 1970. Successive Governments tried and largely failed to curb the runaway power of unions in the era. It wasn't until Thatcher took on the NUM in 1984 that the tide was truly turned against them.

Union power in the 1970s was absolute.

There hardly seemed to be any business that wasn't prepared to down tools when there were issues to be fought over.

Even the staff of the nearby Fiesta cabaret club in Sheffield walked out in 1976 - Conisbrough crooner Tony Christie had to cross picket lines to perform!

In 1971 postal workers went on strike for the first time ever.

But nothing compared to the miners' strike of January 1972. They came out in protest against a £2-a-week pay offer by the National Coal Board.

The miners were well organised and the Government ill prepared (unlike Thatcher who stockpiled coal in readiness for a strike the following decade).

By the middle of February 1972 the miners had succeeded in shutting 14 power stations because of coal shortages.

The actions were unprecedented. Backed

Whitworth Show Committee
1976 MISS WHITWORTH CONTEST
DISCO
Friday, June 25, from 8 p.m.
Whitworth Institute Ballroom
ADMISSION 20p
Winner will receive £10 and Goward Rose Bowl
Two Runners-up: £5 each
Girls of 15 years and over (by June 25) are invited to enter this year's competition. Just come along on the evening — no entry forms required

into a corner, the Conservative Government under Prime Minister Edward Heath declared a state of emergency, and a three-day-week ensued.

The miners returned to work and the state of emergency was lifted a few days later but union issues were by no means over.

The Government introduced a statutory price and incomes policy as inflation was running at a staggering 25 per cent. But in May 1973 the powerful TUC called a strike against it and got the support of 1.6 million workers.

Though the situation started to ease in the summer, things took another turn in the direction of crisis because of the Arab-Israeli war which was causing a worldwide oil shortage and soaring prices at the pumps.

Petrol ration books were issued and a 50mph speed limit introduced.

The miners, choosing the moment when Prime Minister Heath was at his most vulnerable, then demanded a pay increase of more than the Government maximum. The miners also introduced an overtime ban and power and railway workers quickly followed suit.

In December another three-day-week was introduced; if shops wanted to open on non-electricity days they were free to do so but had to use lamps or candles for lighting...

Television programmes ended at 10.30pm to encourage people to go to bed!

Libby Jones said: "I have two abiding memories: being a hairdresser and having customers sitting in semi-darkness with wet hair in rollers waiting for the power to come back on so they could get under the dryer and at home boiling a kettle on the open coal fire to make up my baby's feed!"

Malcolm Sergeant said: "As a trainee engineer in the mid-1970s, I remember changing a toilet roll when working at our Chesterfield factory and being seriously worried that someone might find out and accuse me of doing somebody else's job! My predecessor had almost caused a strike by helping to sweep up some rubbish. The union's grip was total and the atmosphere was poisonous. I don't agree with all that Margaret Thatcher did, but I can't deny something had to be done."

Caroline Jordan said: "Crazy days! I remember the three-day-week; we had to go to school in groups, all wearing luminous yellow bands on our coat sleeves so that we could be seen in the dark. Then we'd come home and huddle round the gas cooker for heat. Then there was the heatwave in '76 when we had severe thunderstorms and water shortages. I developed my love of ice cream that year! The winter of discontent caused a lot of disruption through all the strike action but to a teenager who cared for little else but music, fashion and boys, most of the politics just passed me by! I do have fond memories of the seventies, but then I didn't have any worries or responsibilities."

Nancy's Motor Spares of Whit Moor

Courtesy of Derbyshire Library Service and www.picturethepast.org.uk

A town turns out for the Queen

The visit of the Queen and Prince Philip in her Jubilee year was a massive event for Chesterfield.

It was the Queen's first ever visit to the town and it took place on Thursday, July 28, 1977.

Much of the visit was organised by the Chesterfield Town Hall and it was all back to theirs at 1pm for a luncheon.

Nothing was left to chance. The Queen had let it be known that she'd be turning up in a hat so the Town Hall said "it is expected that all ladies will also wear hats".

And just in case any of the gents got confused and gave Prince Philip a curtsy there were instructions aplenty to keep them on the straight and narrow.

The Town Hall instructions read: "On being presented, each lady will be expected to curtsy to Her Majesty but in the case of the Duke of Edinburgh no curtsy is expected, and a handshake will be all that is required. In the case of gentlemen, they will bow both to Her Majesty and to the Duke of Edinburgh. The bow should be from the shoulder and not from the waist."

Town Hall steward, Mr G Allen (right) meets the Queen

Crowds gather for the Queen's visit

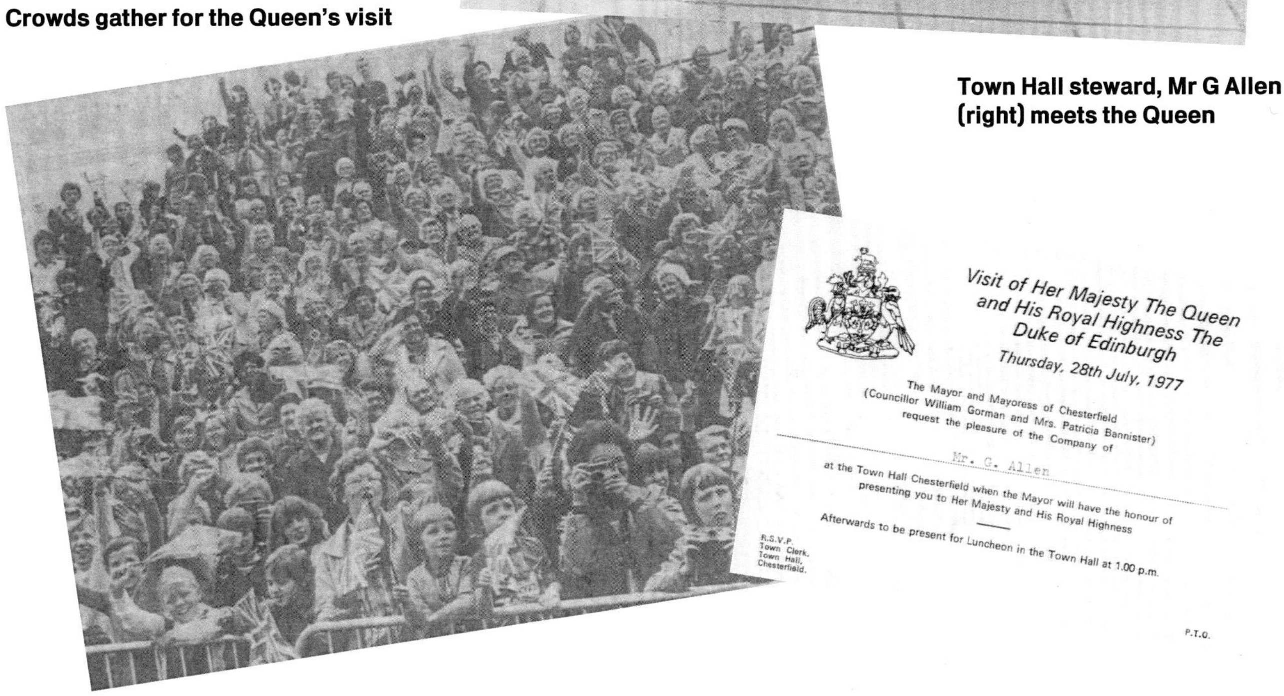

Visit of Her Majesty The Queen and His Royal Highness The Duke of Edinburgh

Thursday, 28th July, 1977

The Mayor and Mayoress of Chesterfield
(Councillor William Gorman and Mrs. Patricia Bannister)
request the pleasure of the Company of

Mr. G. Allen

at the Town Hall Chesterfield when the Mayor will have the honour of presenting you to Her Majesty and His Royal Highness

Afterwards to be present for Luncheon in the Town Hall at 1.00 p.m.

R.S.V.P.
Town Clerk,
Town Hall,
Chesterfield.

P.T.O.

The Shakespeare - a pub that was razed to the ground to make way for the 'donut' car park. (you'll also notice the traffic traveled the other way those days)

Painted Wagon - a firm favourite of the era

POLICE ADVICE

How to guard against bomb attacks

THE CHIEF CONSTABLE of Derbyshire, Mr. Walter Stansfield, held a seminar at Force Headquarters, Butterley, on Tuesday, to which senior executives of commerce, industry and local government in the county, were invited to discover ways to help guard against bomb or incendiary attacks and possible letter bombs.

Among the hints relating to bomb and incendiary attacks are:

- Secure open basement areas and supervise access to underground parking or loading bays, restrict parking to an area away from the building.
- Secure doors and windows, illuminate porches and basement areas, leave ground floor lights on at night, remove ladders, paint drainpipes with anti-climb paint, secure skylights and other roof access points, install intruder alarms and employ guards or night watchmen.
- Secure doors and windows giving access to fuel storage and central heating plants and boilers. Check fire fighting equipment and fire escapes.
- Restrict public access areas.
- Warn staff to be alert for anybody entering carrying a parcel, case or similar object, especially if they try to leave without it.
- Fit grilles, bandit glass or other materials to protect staff.
- Use polycarbonate sheets to reduce casualties from flying glass or fit Venetian blinds or some other window protection.
- Check the buildings after working hours to make sure no-one is hiding before locking up.
- Have someone who is familiar with the appearance and contents of each office or department to do a check so that suspect packages can be spotted.

Police say that anyone with any suspicions about any object should not touch it but should contact the police immediately.

Go-go dancers went hand in hand with the early 1970s

David Jacobs a guest of the ladies

Guest speaker David Jacobs pictured in hi... with, left to right, Mrs. Margaret Meeney (Treasurer), Dr. Jean Nettleship (Cha... ...Robinson (Secretary).

TELEVISION personality David Jacobs was guest of honour at the sixth annual dinner of Chesterfield Ladies' Luncheon Club last week at the Station Hotel, Chesterfield.

The Loyal Toas... posed by the Ch... Jean Nettleship... toastmaster was... Rice.

Mrs. Pat Rice... vote of thanks...

Aquarius regular Bernard Manning and friends

The Crown & Cushion

Another '70s 'selfie'

Looking towards the Pomegranate Theatre of today

The Shambles in the late 1960s

CHAPTER FOUR

SUNBATHING IN QUEENS PARK - THE SUMMER OF '76

Queens Park

The year 1976 has come out on top as the best year ever on a couple of occasions in recent years.

It got the thumbs up from the New Economics Foundation as the most favourable 12 months for quality of life whilst a 2012 study said it was voted best year to have a child.

Anyone growing up in Chesterfield at that point probably remembers it for one thing and one thing only - the scorching weather!

The summer seemed to go on forever as day after day pushed the thermometer into the 90s and the flares were rolled up for a spot of sunbathing in Queens Park.

But it wasn't all sweetness and light in the year; especially in the pop charts.

For some it was bemoaned as the year the music died as the likes of Elton John and Abba were shunned in favour of anarchy-charged young upstarts like the Sex Pistols and The Clash.

The sun didn't help our sporting prowess much either; England were hammered by the Aussies at cricket and the much publicised athletics team limped home from the Montreal Olympics with just one bronze medal between them.

Thankfully racing ace James Hunt saved the day by winning the Formula One championship.

Other highlights/lowlights of the year of unfeasibly hot sun included Brotherhood of Man, the Muppet Show on TV and James Callaghan as PM.

Even house-brick-style mobile phones were a long way off - at this point only half of UK households had a landline.

Whilst the youth drank flagons of Mansfield Marksman lager to keep cool there was more

than a bit of a downside to the unprecedented heat; a drought led to thousands of people across the country being dependent on standpipes for their water supply.

There was even a Minister of Drought, Denis Howell, who was quickly nicknamed 'Minister of Floods' when the heavens finally opened, and open they did!

It was also a year of strikes, no real surprise there, and raging inflation once again.

In fact the scale of the economic failure was laid bare with the country forced to ask international bankers to bail it out to the spectacular tune of a billion pounds.

It would only take a couple more years of industrial unrest and economic chaos and the stage was set to enable Margaret Thatcher to take up the post of Prime Minister in 1979.

Edward Lord: "I don't know what you mean - 1976 was a fabulous year for music. I saw the Clash make their live debut in Sheffield at the Black Swan supporting the Sex Pistols!"

Ian Faulder: "It was great for an 11-year-old like I was. I spent the entire summer holiday outside - what was the point of being inside with only 3 TV Channels which mainly showed a test card during the day! No computers, no mobiles, no designer rip-off clothes and no money to buy them anyway The single most valuable and sought after object for someone my age was my Raleigh Chopper or my brothers smaller Tomahawk! I wouldn't trade that time for growing up nowadays."

Jane Sugden: "I remember the arrival of Swap Shop on TV screens in 1976. The road show arrived in Chesterfield a year or two after. It was in Queens Park one Saturday morning. It was absolutely rammed. I remember Cheggers charging around swapping all this stuff. It was total chaos but very enjoyable!"

Paul Shaw: "We couldn't afford a car for a while so went everywhere on my motorbike. Luckily for us the summer of 1976 was made for bikers! The 1970s must be the decade of the worst cars ever - the Marina, the Allegro and the Viva. A friend bought a brand new Rover 3500. It broke down within half a mile of the dealer. The joke at the time was that the dealer had to have each new owner followed around by a breakdown crew in a Mercedes van - the British vans weren't reliable enough!"

The Market Hall

Matlock Bath was a hit with the bikers in the '70s - somethings never change

Courtesy of Chesterfield Photographic Society and www.picturethepast.org.uk

Littlewoods was a mainstay of town centre retail for years

The death of Elvis sent shockwaves through the rock'n'roll community

Chesterfield had a wealth of busy Working Men's Clubs

Into the bitter battle...

THE LADIES NOTCH UP A RESOUNDING VICTORY FOR WOMEN'S (HIC) LIB

By a staff reporter

THERE was standing room only in the lounge bar of the Horse and Groom, Glosstone, last night, as regulars crowded into the pub to see the contest of the year . . .

A beer battle of the sexes!

Mother-of-four, Mrs. Mary Grayson, of Overend Way, and 21-year-old barmaid, Susan Taylor, of Middlebay Close, had decided to challenge the old husbands' tale that beer was a man's drink by taking on the combined skill of two local lads in a yard of ale drinking contest.

And the result — A bitter defeat for the men.

LADIES FIRST

After winning the toss, 27-year-old Tony Cartwright, of Blackstock Road, and 25-year-old Ernest Lazenby, of Overend Drive, put the ladies in to drink first.

Before the drinking started the audience was told that the world record for the event was a staggering 6½ seconds.

The ladies did not quite manage to equal that, but quaffed their yard — equal to 2½ pints — in a very respectable 2 mins. 5 secs., without spilling a drop.

Then came the men's turn. They began well and looked likely to break the ladies' time.

But then, near the end of the yard, they seemed to reach their limit and could not let victory slip down their throats.

[illegible] of the male contenders had ever tried yard of ale drinking before. One of the women had, and this MUST have affected the result.

And for the women? "We were only here for the beer, and it was lovely," said 41-year-old Mrs. Grayson.

The contest was organised by licensee Mr. Will Cambell to raise money for Muscular Dystrophy Research, and next weekend a tug-of-war race has been arranged across Blackstock Road.

Mrs. Grayson also took part in a pram race last Sunday which raised £10 for the same charity, but the doll's pram she was travelling in collapsed under her 12½ stone weight only yards from the starting line.

Winners of the race were Stuart Grafton and Tony Cartwright, Ernest Lazenby and Brian Lambert were second and Derek and Frank Boyce, from the nearby Wyvern Hotel pub, third, with Malcolm Blackshaw and Mrs. Madge Sheldon fourth. Last night the winners received their prizes from parish Jennifer Handley.

Mrs. Sheldon and Mrs. Grayson received consolation prizes. Mrs. Sheldon provided a fashion show interlude during the evening.

The moneyraising efforts at the pub are for a national competition organised among pubs throughout [illegible]

●MRS. Mary Grayson on the winning trail in her effort to sink a yard of ale in the drinking contest.

MEN DO THEIR BEST, BUT IT JUST IS NOT GOOD ENOUGH

[illegible] with partner Ernest Lazenby do their [illegible] for the men.

OUT TO PROVE THAT THEY'RE ONLY THERE FOR THE BEER

● MRS. Mary Grayson (left) helps her partner, Susan Taylor, to support the yard glass.

Tying the knot at North Wingfield Church

Manor School pupils hard at work in Ms Freeman's music lesson (the author is second from the left)

Finding acts to provide entertainment seven nights a week for venues like the Aquarius and Sheffield Fiesta was no easy job

It was a rare thing but men occasionally did the weekly shop in the era

CHAPTER FIVE

ADAM & EVE SERVES UP T-BONE STEAK WITH ITS DANCE FLOOR

CFC Chairman Dave Allen (centre) who owned the town's Adam & Eve

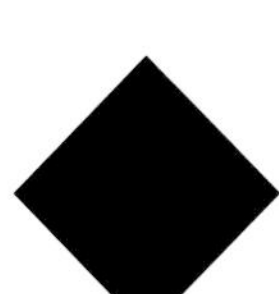

These days he's better known as the chairman of Chesterfield Football Club.

In December 1971 he was the 20-something entrepreneur that had just opened the second of what went onto to be a chain of Adam & Eve venues.

The first was in Leicester, the second transformed the former bowling alley on Lordsmill Street in Chesterfield.

Dave Allen ploughed £40,000 into the venture - a hefty sum in 1971.

"When we opened we had a nice 40-seater restaurant and live acts on a Friday and Saturday night. We were very top end. No jeans and a smart casual dress code", he said.

"You could get T-bone steak, scampi or chicken. People came from far and wide; Matlock, the Amber Valley and Dronfield.

"It would be ladies/nurses night on a Wednesday, half price beer on a Tuesday and hen parties on a Thursday."

But the Adam & Eve wasn't Dave Allen's first taste of success in Chesterfield. He actually brought a mobile disco to the Victoria Ballroom and got a feel for the town and its audiences.

"I knew there was potential after that. I then had to seek out the right premises."

Wrestler Alan Kilby worked the door at the Adam & Eve and CFC players would regularly be in attendance. Pernod would be drunk with lemonade or orange and it would be a G&T for anyone with ideas above their station.

DJs included the likes of Pat Sweetwater and Noddy.

The Adam & Eve became a cornerstone of Chesterfield's evening economy for the

duration of the era.

Starting out at the YMCA

Dave Stone: "The YMCA was the place the 13 and 14 year olds went for their first piece of romance. There'd be a disco and ages would go right up to 17 and 18. There'd rarely be any trouble.

"The schools must have got on better then as I went to Tapton but we were still welcome at the Grammar School disco.

"There was also the fun of the open air swimming pool on Stand Road. I remember the little changing huts. It was always cold!

"As we got older we'd start going to pubs like the Terminus and the Portland. The Woodside was quite popular as well and there were some big disco nights at the Bradbury.

"When you met in town at night it was always on Stephenson Place or outside Co-Op on Elder Way.

"I used to play in a band, Rio 5, and I'd spend every spare hour in Hudsons music shop.

"Some Kinda Mushroom on Newbold Road was the place for records and second hand albums.

"The Blue Bell at Bolsover was popular for bands, Divy the landlord, who was also a part time fireman, booked a lot of rock bands. It was the place for bikers and good bands.

"Hollingwood Hotel had a function room upstairs which had bands on. There was also the Black Rock at Cromford and the ever popular Brim Tavern.

"There was a very thriving scene. The Working Men's Clubs were always really packed and Rio 5 could easily work five or six nights a week.

"Working Men's Clubs were always interesting at the weekend. It was family night on the Saturday, Sunday lunch was mostly males as there were strippers on and Sunday night was a more an elder audience.

"There were two versions of Rio 5; one rockier and another version fronted by one Bridey Kerr.

"I was also a roadie for a band called Pelican later known as Odinstorm. I used to go to the Brimington Tavern most nights for their rock nights where a number of local bands played like Chalky White, Vesuvius and Odinstorm played on a regular basis.

"Painted Wagon was very popular in Chesterfield. It didn't get really rough until the 1980s."

A night in Chesterfield

Like many, Linda Jean Stevens has nothing but fond memories of a night on the tiles in the 1970s

"My memories of going out in Chesterfield in the '70s are of great fun, and, compared to today, very little trouble. The police certainly didn't have to be out in force as they are today! Everybody seemed to know each other and we didn't seem to have to get drunk! A typical Friday night..(that was THE main night to be out) would be: meet at The Market Hotel first.. That was a very popular place back then, full of friends. Then spent considerable time in the Painted Wagon... Always busy in there and they played great music.

"After pubs closed at 11pm we were off down to the Adam and Eve until 2am. That was all about the dancing! The Adam and Eve was home from home really, we knew everyone. They had cheap drink nights in the week. People came from far and wide to the Eve... It was a great nightspot. I remember people telling me they preferred Chesterfield nightlife to any other in the surrounding area! I remember, at Easter and for religious reasons, they weren't allowed to open on Good Friday until after midnight (taking it into the Saturday) so we would have to wait around for another hour after pub closure, until they were allowed to open their doors! Then they stayed open until 4am! It didn't put anyone off... Still packed. We went to Jingles on a Thursday night. That was very popular also... Totally different atmosphere to the Eve and a great dance floor. Probably because it had a lot of history behind it. They used to have pop star nights occasionally too. I remember seeing Tina Charles there.

"When the Aquarius opened, well, the town had never seen anything like it. A very "big city" feel to it. Good shows, great acts, two dance floors. We didn't go there every week... More for special occasions... A lot of people did though. I worked for a GP practice in town and so we got to join in The Royal Hospital outings regularly. Every so often they would arrange a night out to Nottingham, Sheffield or Derby. Usually The Palais Nottingham, The Pink Coconut Derby, and anywhere in Sheffield... Give me Chesterfield any day!! Fashions... Well. I remember loud shirts, afro hair, flares but it wasn't as awful as they make out now... They exaggerate!! The music was brilliant in the '70s...

"We lived through a really great era....From Motown to funk...fantastic to dance to! Most clothes bought from Bobby Cousins, High Street, Etams or Osbourns stall, Chesterfield Market! A popular Hair Salon was Croppers which was only a portacabin at the back of Knifesmithgate, but brilliant. Records from either Hudson's or Boots... Or you could to get ex jukebox records occasionally."

Looking towards Lordsmill Roundabout

Courtesy of Hasland Hall Community School. and www.picturethepast.org.uk

The Market Hall

Courtesy of Chesterfield Photographic Society and www.picturethepast.org.uk

Looking towards Eyres - a cornerstone of the town's retail since records began (well, a long time anyway)

The mighty Adam & Eve complete, on this occasion, with an icon of '70s Britain, the Raleigh Chopper

Vicar Lane's Red Lion - a long gone legend

Chesterfield's Co-op department store was thriving in the era

A bit of seventies-style TLC for the Crooked Spire

JINGLES MAKES WAY FOR THE FUSION

Demand for vinyl was unprecedented with CDs years away

The sheer number and variety of venues on offer in 1970s Chesterfield dwarfs anything we have today: cabaret club, discotheques, pubs, restaurants, wine bars, Working Men's Clubs, cinemas and even out-of-town nightclubs like nearby Fanny's at Owler Bar.

Licensing laws couldn't have been more different. No all day, all night, bars in the era. As pubs shut the nightclubs opened - end of.

One venue that didn't last long into the 1980s was the Fusion (or Jingles as it was better known by many). These days it's better known as part of the Winding Wheel complex but in the 1970s it was a very popular nightspot.

Lynn Jones remembers her nights in the era: "I started working at Eyre's furniture store in the office the day before my 16th birthday which was July 1974. I remember buying a 3 piece navy blue trouser suit from a colleague's catalogue which cost me £1.12 a week, as I only earned about £7.50 this was a lot! I remember wearing it at the Aquarius to see the Grumbleweeds.

"Chesterfield Market was really buzzing in the '70s; there was a clothes stall called Ozzy's which we thought was fab, and we bought lots of stuff from there; Bobby Cousins, on the High St, was probably the only boutique at that time in Chesterfield.

"Pubs in Chesterfield were the Painted Wagon, which was the in place to go; we used to drink Colt 45 which came in a small can, what was that all about? The Painted Wagon used to have a kind of circle in the middle with stairs up to the sides, lots of girls used to just walk around up one side then down the other, we called them floor walkers.

"Other pubs were the Market, Gardeners, Whites, and Crooked Spire.

"Nightclubs were Jingles

which then became Fusion, I can vaguely remember Jingles, having a downstairs bar with pouffes in brown and white...

"Also we went to the Aquarius and had chicken and chips in a basket, and the Adam and Eve, we used to go to the rock night which was on a Monday night. How we got up for work the next day I have no idea. I remember head banging to 'Free Bird' by Lynyrd Skynyrd and 'Because the Night' by Patti Smith.

"I was 21 in 1979 and had a party at Tupton Village Hall. We did all the catering - lovely buffet!!!

"I had a 3-in-1 record player, cassette deck and radio for my 21st and had Meat Loaf 'Bat Out Of Hell', Kate Bush think it was the 'Kick Inside', and Blondie 'Parallel Lines' LP's!"

Mick Spracklen: I remember going to Jingles every Thursday night when I was about 14. A mate used to pay the night shift their wages down at Tube Works at 9.30pm and then leg it back up town just in time because our free tickets were for latest 10pm entry. Stay there till 2pm and go to school next day smelling like a brewery. Ha ha. If I remember correctly, there was a small round dance floor with 4 tall drinks tables positioned round the outside

Me and Baby Brother - 'War' and 'Purple Haze' - Jimi Hendrix used to be played a lot.

Diane Okeefe: "I used to go in late '70s when it changed to Fusion."

Jane Kirk: "Had my handbag nicked twice at Jingles. First one found upstairs in toilet cistern in ladies toilet. The second never found only a pint pot found at the bottom of the steps of emergency exit where we had been stood. Must say our bags where a lot safer when we were dancing round them. lol"

Linda Jean Stevens: "Dancing round the handbags, memories!!! Don't see it anymore, they laugh when you tell them about that now!! lol

Stars of the future graced the Fusion first

Nightlife is pretty cyclic in the way fashions come and go but there's little, certainly not on the chart front, that can touch a brief window in 1979.

The calibre of artists found to be playing Thursday nights at the Fusion were quite astounding for a Northern town hardly renowned for its place on the national gig circuit.

Even Sheffield's Limit club, which was going full tilt at this point, had a run for its money.

Chatsworth Road in an era when the cappuccino was still a frothy glint in the greasy spoon owner's eye

Thanks have to be given to promoter Stuart Smith who ran the town's Connection Records.

He said in an interview with Toy Town Times fanzine in the early 1980s: "At the end of 1978 the local music scene was pretty much in the same state as it is today; bad. A lot of older folk were only too keen to tell you about seeing Jimi Hendrix at the ABC or Pink Floyd at St James Hall; and all the groups that appeared at the Vic Ballroom (now Supa Q) read like rock's who's who. This was great if you were around in the '60s but to us it meant nothing."

In March 1979 posters started appearing around Chesterfield detailing the start of something new for a Thursday night.

The Cure headlined the first night, April 5, 1979. Nearly 400 were in attendance. A big improvement on the 30 or so that were turning up to regular Thursday nights at the Fusion.

The roster over the following seven months was quite incredible and included a host of acts that went on to national and international fame including the Specials, Simple Minds, the Pretenders, Def Leppard and the Cure (they returned in June).

APRIL 5 - 1979 - THE CURE - First time they played they were really good - played five encores including 'Killing An Arab' at least three times.
APRIL 12 - DOLL BY DOLL - Much hyped at the time - but still good although they played a bit too loud for comfort. Support band was Spasms.
APRIL 19 - STRAY KAT - A local blues band - The Adam & Eve was closed that night and the Fusion crowd was nearly 500 strong.
APRIL 26 - NEGATIVES - 226 people payed to see two members of a Sheffield group who later became Yah-Boo.
MAY 3 - PRESSURE SHOCKS - This gig was a real strange one - The group smoked their heads off in the dressing room and wouldn't appear until very late - When they did come on this Derby reggae group were v.good. Atmosphere was good with most of the audience dancing to da reggae sound.
MAY 10 - WITCHFYNDE - Heavy group comes to Fusion - a lot of the regulars passed on this one but over 300 folks turned up.
MAY 17 - THOMPSON TWINS - Big return for local group who played most of their gigs in Sheffield - sounding like X.T.C. the Twins got little response from the punters.
MAY 24 - NEON -
MAY 30 - PUNISHMENT OF LUXURY - By all accounts this was a good gig.
JUNE 7 - 2.3 - Brought in at the last moment. 2.3 a local Sheffield group provided good entertainment.
JUNE 14 - THE CURE - Second time around the Cure were already going downhill.
JUNE 21 - VOYAGER - A BAD mistake by the promoter.
JUNE 28 - ERIC BELL - Another rock act - this one - an ex Thin Lizzy guitarist - played a twenty minute version of 'Whiskey In Jar' to stress the fact.

JULY 5 - 1979 - COMSAT ANGELS - Another Sheffield group who went onto bigger success although on this performance it wasn't obvious that they were going to make it.
JULY 12 SIMPLE MINDS - Only 234 people witnessed this great gig. Most of Chesterfield being too slow to catch a cold.
JULY 19 THE SPECIALS - Perhaps the best night ever at Fusion. At the time the Specials were on the verge of big success with 'Gangsters'.
JULY 26 THE PRETENDERS - Very disappointing cos as a live group they just couldn't cut it. Even Chrissie Hynde wasn't so good looking close up.
AUG. 2 THE ZONES - Scottish group who were O.K. but nothing more.
AUG. 9 ANGELIC UPSTARTS - could they really have been that bad and that ugly ?
AUG. 16 INVADERS - Boring.
Aug. 23 FIXER - The highlight or lowlight was the drummer who after his solo ran around the crowd and dropped his trousers.
Aug. 30 DEF LEPPARD - 350 people saw band who are now millionaires.
Sept. 6 THE SPASMS - headline night for local boys who are now much improved as The Circus.
Sept. 13 THE CHORDS - It took me one night to find out that the mod revival was going nowhere. In other words the Chords were crap and they spoilt a good night where all the audience was dressed up in 60's period piece.
Sept. 20 PHIL RAMBOW - Good act but badly supported.
Sept. 27 THE SELECTER - Inferior version of the Specials.
Oct. 1 PIRATES - Three old men who certainly knew how to rock'n'roll.
Oct. 11 PUNILUX - Fusion favourites - 'Jellyfish' being a dancefloor hit.
Oct. 19 MEKONS - Three people clapped.
Oct. 26 LEW LEWIS - Final night for groups - THE END OF AN ERA...

How Stuart Smith summed up his Fusion Thursday night gigs a few years after in local fanzine, Toytown Times

The hallowed entrance to the Fusion, months after it shut its doors for the last time

The Cure and Doll By Doll rock the Fusion

Youths spent night with pigs after stolen drink spree

AFTER drinking a large quantity of alcohol which they had stolen from the Anvil Club at Ironville, three youths spent the night in a barn with some pigs, it was stated at Alfreton Juvenile Court on Friday.

The youths — two 16-year-olds from Ironville, and a 15-year-old from Riddings — admitted entering Ironville Church Hall and stealing drinks worth £6 6s 3d. The Ironville youths were each fined £10, and the third youth was ordered to spend 12 hours at an attendance centre.

Mr Keith Malkin, prosecuting, said that the Anvil Club was a licensed club run at Ironville Church Hall.

[illegible]

empty bottles, which had apparently come from the church hall.

When the youths were seen they made statements admitting that they had got into the hall, taken the drinks — "and consumed them rapidly with most unfortunate and unpleasant results."

One of the statements described how two of the youths went into the hall in the early hours of the morning, and handed out the bottles to the third one. Then they went to a shed and drank the alcohol. When rain started coming into the shed they went into a nearby barn and spent the night in the company of pigs.

[illegible]

A trip to the East Coast was essential entertainment for area's youth

Cars had multiple uses for the ever inventive youth

The skinhead fashion of the seventies

From Jingles to the Fusion

Nobody was closer to the major artists playing the Fusion than Martin Edwards.

He said: "It was my job to look after the Pretenders and get them on and off the stage. It was a very big coup to get them there.

"It was a very busy venue. I started there around 1975 when it was called Jingles. It was owned by Top Rank. I became one of the door staff.

"I remember Wednesday used to be a very good night. There were a lot of theme nights and promotional nights. It would be open Wednesday to Saturday. It was around 500 capacity.

"It shut for around a month to be freshened up and reopened as the Fusion. It was good - we still got paid for the time it was shut!

"I ended up leaving the Fusion because the crowds got increasingly hard to control.

"I remember what a great night Christmas Eve used to be. Lunch time would be absolutely packed."

As well as being a member of the nightclub door staff, Martin was also a day time employee of the Co-op in Chesterfield in the era. He has fond memories.

"They used to lay on a Co-op train for staff to take them on a day trip to Skegness or Blackpool. There was even a beer carriage. It was one big party train!

"I remember one year we missed the train back from Blackpool. We ended up having to get another train to Manchester Victoria, then another to Manchester Piccadilly, another to Sheffield and finally a taxi to Chesterfield. We got back at 6am and had to be back at work for 9am. Happy days!"

Hoardings on the right around the site of the new police station

This Star newspaper reporter didn't exactly help dispel the image of misinformed fashion in the era by sporting this little number

The Hare & Greyhound

Derby Road protest

CHAPTER SEVEN

ALL GLAMMED UP FOR THURSDAY NIGHT TOTP

No look defined the seventies better than the stack-heeled, glittering image of glam rock.

Whilst the parents got more and more depressed thanks to the daily news diet of inflation, industrial disputes and general social unrest; the kids were more than happy to bide their time until their weekly fill of Top of the Pops on a Thursday night arrived.

It was then down to the stars of the day to go head-to-head to see who could conjure up the most showstopping, outlandish attire.

Things didn't get much bigger, or madder, than mid-afternoon on December 25, 1973, when the nation's glam rocking youth crammed round the TV for the biggest event of the year, the Christmas edition of Top of the Pops.

Masters of ceremony for the tinsel-charged edition were Messrs Blackburn and Edmunds and they'd barely got their introductions out the way before Slade swaggered onto the stage to tear through 'Cum On Feel The Noize'.

They really could do no wrong. 'Merry Xmas Everybody' had become the band's third

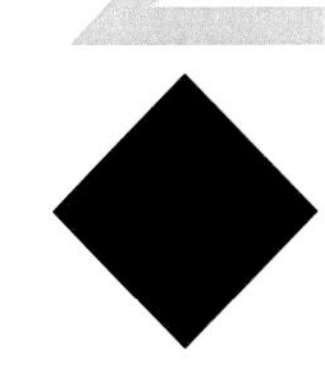

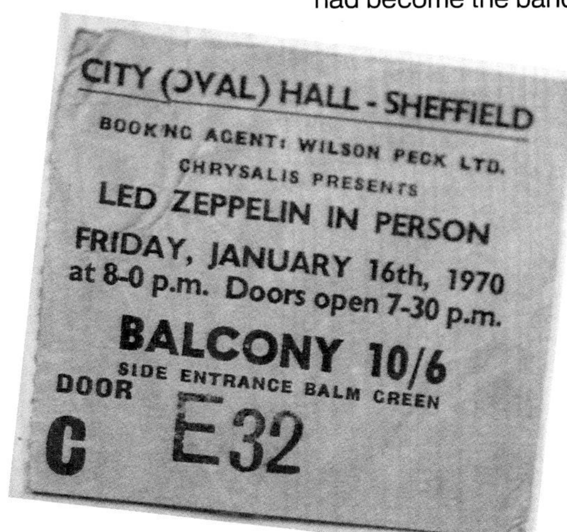

CITY (OVAL) HALL - SHEFFIELD
BOOKING AGENT: WILSON PECK LTD.
CHRYSALIS PRESENTS
LED ZEPPELIN IN PERSON
FRIDAY, JANUARY 16th, 1970
at 8-0 p.m. Doors open 7-30 p.m.
BALCONY 10/6
DOOR SIDE ENTRANCE BALM GREEN
C E32

number one just a few days earlier.

The show also contained the Sweet performing the barnstorming 'Blockbuster', Suzi Quatro with 'Can The Can' and Wizzard with 'See My Baby Jive' and more.

In between the giants of glam, looking almost paltry in comparison, were the likes of Peters and Lee, David Cassidy and Donny Osmond.

There's no doubt the era was one of extremes when it came to music and image.

By the summer of 1976 things were in a state of flux once again with Thin Lizzy flying the rock flag, disco amply represented by the likes of Candi Staton and Tavares and the weighty frame of Demis Roussos proving there's always room for a spanner in the works.

But it was rise of punk rock that really caught people off guard. Pub rock bands like Eddie and the Hot Rods and Dr Feelgood were already smoothing the way but it would take the Sex Pistols to finally make safety pins and bondage trousers de rigueur for aspiring upstarts countrywide.

The nearby Sheffield City Hall was the place to catch most of the chart acts. Everyone from the Bay City Rollers to T-Rex graced the Oval Hall stage. There was also David Bowie and the Spiders from Mars, Lou Reed and host of others.

The Sex Pistols never quite made it. Their 'Anarchy In The UK' tour was booked to play but a ban was put into place before they got chance to get out of the tour bus.

It was a decade that said goodbye to some true music giants; The Beatles split in 1970 and Elvis died in 1977 with Janis Joplin, Jimi Hendrix and Jim Morrison all passing away at the young age of 27 earlier on in the era.

There's no doubt you can thank the 1970s for some of the finest British music ever recorded; Rolling Stones, T-Rex, The Clash, David Bowie and Led Zeppelin. The list of acts at the top of their game seemed almost unprecedented.

Sheffield City Hall memories

Chris Wintle: "I remember Queen supporting Mott The Hoople. You just knew they were going to be massive - they were fantastic. I remember them doing 'Brighton Rock' - I'd already heard the hype but they were worth even more than that."

Dave Shaw: "I remember the night Marc Bolan only did half an hour at Sheffield City Hall there was nearly a riot. He was very late and the gear had arrived late. Angie Bowie was trying to explain how it wasn't their fault. There were all these old guys that were the stewards in their red jackets looking really worried. Thankfully, Angie Bowie managed to calm everyone down."

Kenny Lock: "Who remembers queuing all night for tickets at Sheffield City Hall? I used to do it quite regularly and it was normally the same faces doing it. There was quite a lot of camaraderie around it! It was far better in the summer though..."

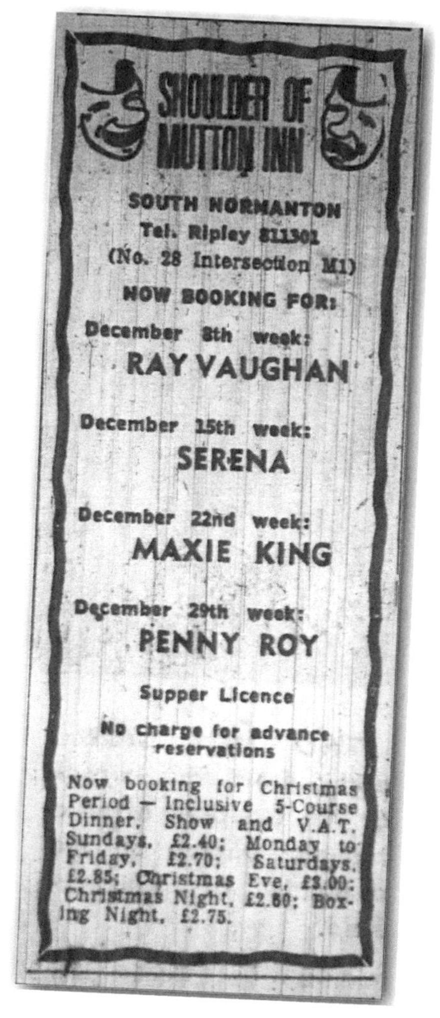

Pracisitng 'back flips' for the Northern Soul dancefloors

Mick Shedd and his Side Effects at The Limit

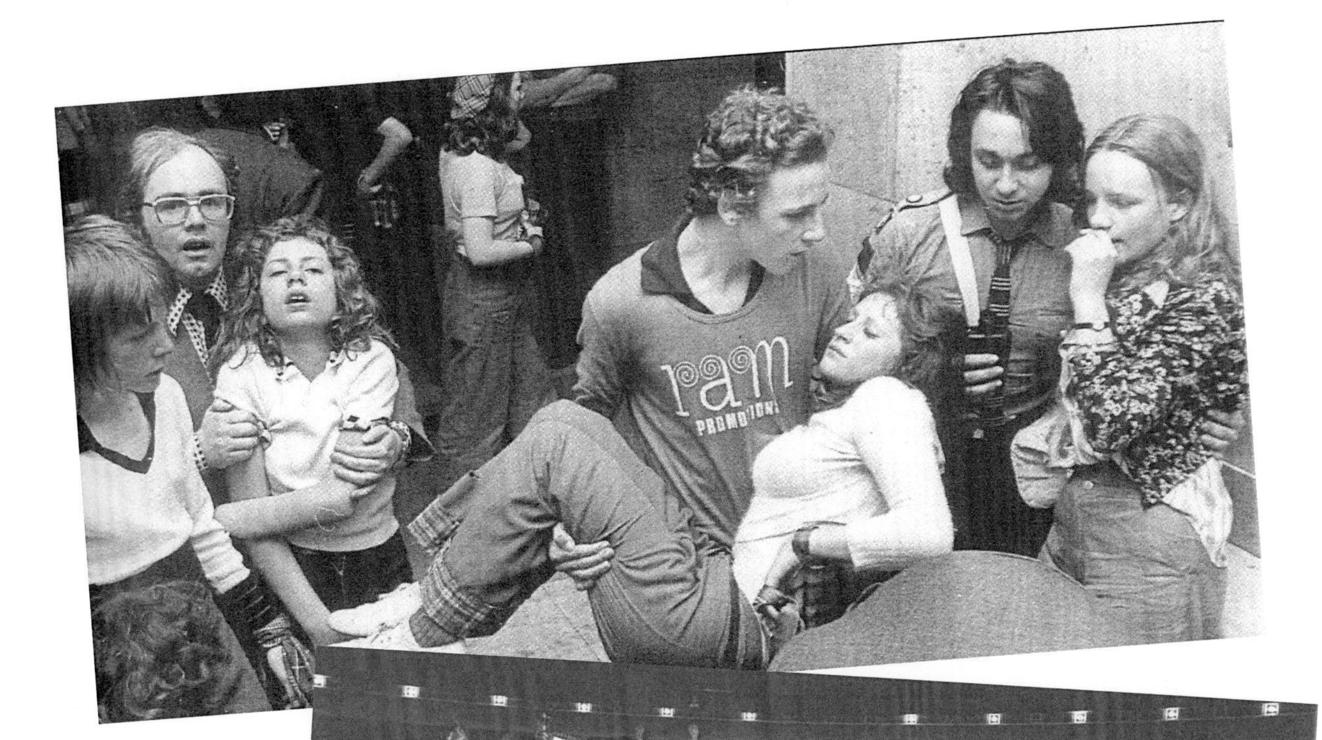

Sheffield City Hall took a while to recover from the Bay City Rollers!

Ladies line up against their Ford Escort

Radio Hallam's 'Big' Ray Stuart interviews Alvin Stardust

Limit club owners Kevan Johnson and George Webster on opening day in 1978 in Sheffield

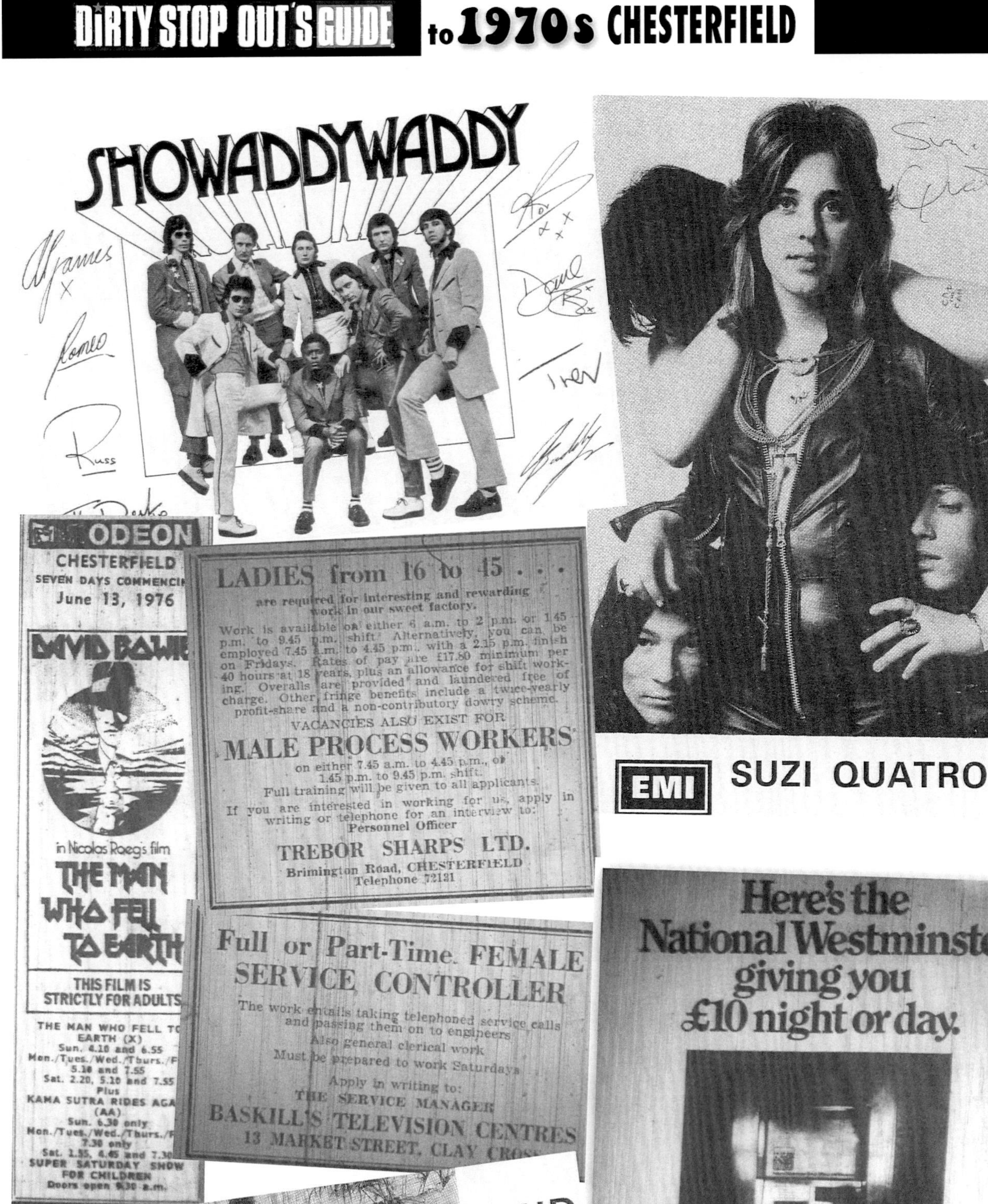

ODEON
CHESTERFIELD
SEVEN DAYS COMMENCING
June 13, 1976

DAVID BOWIE
in Nicolas Roeg's film
THE MAN WHO FELL TO EARTH

THIS FILM IS STRICTLY FOR ADULTS

THE MAN WHO FELL TO EARTH (X)
Sun. 4.10 and 6.55
Mon./Tues./Wed./Thurs./F
5.10 and 7.55
Sat. 2.20, 5.10 and 7.55
Plus
KAMA SUTRA RIDES AGA
(AA)
Sun. 6.30 only
Mon./Tues./Wed./Thurs./F
7.30 only
Sat. 1.55, 4.45 and 7.30
SUPER SATURDAY SHOW FOR CHILDREN
Doors open 9.30 a.m.

LADIES from 16 to 45 . . .

are required for interesting and rewarding work in our sweet factory.

Work is available on either 6 a.m. to 2 p.m. or 1.45 p.m. to 9.45 p.m. shift. Alternatively, you can be employed 7.45 a.m. to 4.45 p.m. with a 2.15 p.m. finish on Fridays. Rates of pay are £17.80 minimum per 40 hours at 18 years, plus an allowance for shift working. Overalls are provided and laundered free of charge. Other fringe benefits include a twice-yearly profit-share and a non-contributory dowry scheme.

VACANCIES ALSO EXIST FOR

MALE PROCESS WORKERS

on either 7.45 a.m. to 4.45 p.m., or 1.45 p.m. to 9.45 p.m. shift.
Full training will be given to all applicants.
If you are interested in working for us, apply in writing or telephone for an interview to:
Personnel Officer

TREBOR SHARPS LTD.
Brimington Road, CHESTERFIELD
Telephone 72121

Full or Part-Time FEMALE SERVICE CONTROLLER

The work entails taking telephoned service calls and passing them on to engineers
Also general clerical work
Must be prepared to work Saturdays
Apply in writing to:
THE SERVICE MANAGER
BASKILL'S TELEVISION CENTRES
13 MARKET STREET, CLAY CROSS

MUD

RA

RECOF

Here's the National Westminster giving you £10 night or day.

This is one of the National Westminster's dispensers.
If you're a customer, just ask your local branch for a special cash card.
Then, whenever you run short of money, you just pop your card into a dispenser, tap out your number, and out come ten crisp notes.
It's all part of the service of Britain's most local bank.
Most local, because we have more branches than any other bank—so there's

We have cash dispensers all over the country, but the ones on *your* doorstep are outside the following banks:

Burton-on-Trent: 166 High Street. **Chesterfield**: 89 New Square. **Derby**: 28 Iron Gate. **Mansfield**: Market Place. **Nottingham**: 1 Angel Row; 37 Friar Lane.

Why not get the National Westminster Bank working 24 hours a day, 7 days a week, for you? Just drop into your local branch and ask about opening an account.

National Westminster Bank

Sex Pistols at Radio Hallam

Siouxsie and the Banshees were the first big band to perform at Sheffield's Limit

CHAPTER EIGHT

SOFT PORN, CHARITY DRINKING MATCHES AND A WORLD BEREFT OF POLITICAL CORRECTNESS

Cornershops were thriving in the era

Whilst the punks turned veggie and imploded in the 1980s, equal opps ruled the 1990s and the politically correct brigade largely took over 21st century England; things were rather more chilled out in the seventies.

Nightlife in the region, in some parts at least, was something on a par with The Sweeney on crack - anything went.

Whilst most industries seemed to be on permanent strike and spent most of the decade holding placards on picket lines, the after dark sector got more and more industrious.

It certainly didn't let incidental issues like blackouts, piles of rotting rubbish, three day working weeks and a 'Winter of Discontent' get in its way for long.

Dinnertime entertainment could be a far cry from the sandwich and quick wander round town most workers make do with today.

Despite the rise of the feminist movement, you could bag three strippers, topless go-go dancer and free beer for only 5p at Hofbrauhaus on Sheffield's Eyre Street in the era - it was on offer six lunchtimes a week and only a bus ride away.

Closer to home there were weekly strippers at Brim Tavern and a host of Working Men's Clubs.

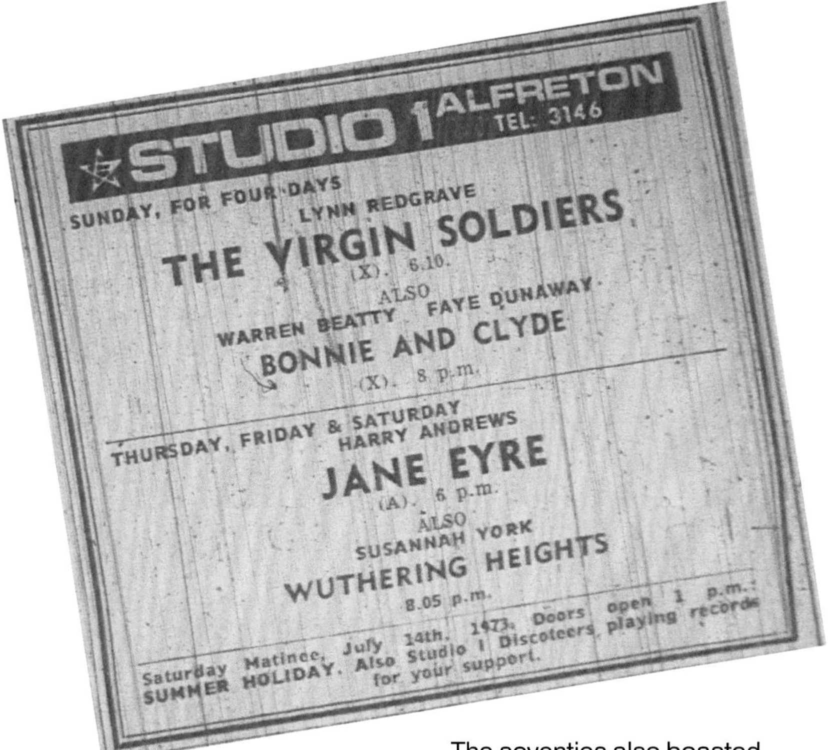

STUDIO 1 ALFRETON TEL: 3146
SUNDAY, FOR FOUR DAYS
LYNN REDGRAVE
THE VIRGIN SOLDIERS
(X). 6.10.
ALSO
WARREN BEATTY FAYE DUNAWAY
BONNIE AND CLYDE
(X). 8 p.m.
THURSDAY, FRIDAY & SATURDAY
HARRY ANDREWS
JANE EYRE
(A). 6 p.m.
ALSO
SUSANNAH YORK
WUTHERING HEIGHTS
8.05 p.m.
Saturday Matinee, July 14th, 1973. Doors open 1 p.m.:
SUMMER HOLIDAY. Also Studio 1 Discoteers playing records for your support.

Women were praised for undertaking marathon drinking sessions in the name of charity and tales of wife swapping parties in nearby Dronfield were front page news.

Chris Twiby said: "The whole country was soft porn and stripping crazy in the seventies.

"Strip shows seemed to operate morning, noon and night and beauty contests were common currency.

"The culture was so different. There was little stigma attached to drinking and driving, smoking was acceptable everywhere and slapping a girl on the backside was taken as a back-handed compliment rather than an immediate disciplinary."

Nightlife entertainment was the perfect way to forget the country's problems via flagons of bitter, Pina Colada chasers and a soft porn flick at the cinema.

The opportunities for partying in seventies Chesterfield were actually far more prevalent than they are now.

A whole generation of pubs and Working Men's Clubs, that were the lifeblood of the 1970s, have gone to the wall in recent years thanks to smoking bans and licensing deregulation.

The seventies also boasted booming beer-offs; Watney Party Seven-packing punters turning up in their droves for house parties and a very up-market social scene that revolved around cocktail parties in the leafy suburbs of Brookside and Walton.

The evening economy was arguably far more booming than it is today and many miss the easily discernible dividing line between pubs and nightclubs of yesteryear.

Chris Twiby said: "There was none of this deregulation lark, allowing bars to nick traditional nightclub trade by opening all night and everyone having to totally restructure their business to survive.

"You knew where you stood in the seventies when the bell rang to call time.

"You were either going to be heralded an after dark hero for downing your drink in one as you headed for a nearby dance floor or you could end up an after dark zero for failing to finish it in time and be banished to the local chippy and then bed."

The social stigma attached to drinking and driving hardly existed in the 1970s - hence venues like the out-of-town Aquarius (though thankfully, there were plenty of buses) nearby Five Ways Motel (which later became Fanny's and is now a rather more sedate hangout in the shape of a cut price carvery) could operate as a popular nightspot with punters driving from miles around.

Mark Shaw said: "Nobody batted an eyelid when anyone drank alcohol and drove in the seventies. It seems absolute madness now. It's doubtful somewhere like Fanny's could exist in 2014. The taxi fares alone would be absolutely astronomical!"

The region certainly wasn't an area to let the grass grow under its feet as far as sexual liberation was concerned.

The allegations of wife swapping parties were confirmed by none other than Rev Richard Sledge, Vicar of Dronfield.

He told The Star at the time: "Yes it exists... It concerns individuals and their families."

The church even ended up offering counselling for its troubled clergy.

The vicar believed the problems stemmed from all-night parties going too far.

He added: "Lots of people have parties at all times of the year. Most parties are just ordinary but why in

some places parties go too far I just don't know."

The vicar went on to say he'd been approached by "remorseful men and women" who'd been involved.

Mother Mary's charity drink success

There was a party of different sort kicking off down the road in nearby Gleadless - a beer battle between the sexes.

Mother-of-four, Mrs Mary Grayson, had decided to play the men at their own game.

She out-drank the lot of them to win the yard of ale competition in record time.

The media at the time billed it as victory for women's lib, in a tongue-in-cheek sort of way.

A recent world record for drinking a yard of ale (approximately two-and-half-pints) stands at five seconds. It's unlikely that record will ever be broken - well not if the local health authority has anything to do with it anyway.

Mary didn't beat the world record that night but we understand she didn't spill a drop and she raised a few quid for charity. Well done mum!

Doug Huntingdon: "Lager was a woman's drink. Men had bitter."

Joanne Stephenson: "Fanny's? It was full of lairy posh people."

John Stephens: "I think there were strippers on two or three times a week at Brim Tavern - it was always heaving. And then there were the Working Men's Clubs of course - strippers were part of the regular line-up. Talk about a different world!" calm everyone down."

First pint in the Punch Bowl

Terry Knowles said: "Storrs Road brill youth club. Met my first love at the YMCA.

"I had my first pint in the Punch Bowl next to the YMCA. I had lime in it thinking mam would not smell it.

"Tried my first Brampton mile at 15-years-old. Got half way. There was about 19 pubs then.

"I've still got my Showaddywaddy teddy boy suit from 1973 - I had it made at Austin Reeds in town."

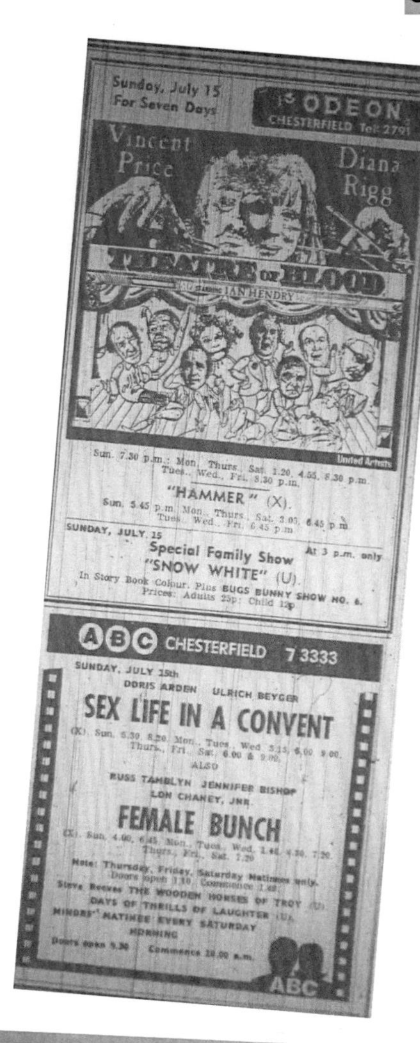
Sunday, July 15
For Seven Days
ODEON
CHESTERFIELD Tel: 2791
Vincent Price
Diana Rigg
THEATRE OF BLOOD
IAN HENDRY
United Artists
Sun. 7.30 p.m.; Mon., Thurs., Sat. 1.20, 4.55, 8.30 p.m.
Tues., Wed., Fri. 8.30 p.m.
"HAMMER" (X).
Sun. 5.45 p.m. Mon., Thurs., Sat. 3.05, 6.45 p.m.
Tues., Wed., Fri. 6.45 p.m.
SUNDAY, JULY 15
Special Family Show At 3 p.m. only
"SNOW WHITE" (U).
In Story Book Colour. Plus BUGS BUNNY SHOW NO. 6.
Prices: Adults 25p; Child 12p

ABC CHESTERFIELD 73333
SUNDAY, JULY 15th
DORIS ARDEN ULRICH BEYGER
SEX LIFE IN A CONVENT
(X). Sun. 5.30, 8.20. Mon., Tues., Wed. 3.15, 6.00, 9.00.
Thurs., Fri., Sat. 6.00 & 9.00.
ALSO
RUSS TAMBLYN JENNIFER BISHOP
LON CHANEY, JNR.
FEMALE BUNCH
(X). Sun. 4.00, 6.45. Mon., Tues., Wed. 1.40, 4.30, 7.20.
Thurs., Fri., Sat. 7.20
Note: Thursday, Friday, Saturday Matinees only.
Doors open 1.10. Commence 1.40.
Steve Reeves THE WOODEN HORSES OF TROY (U).
DAYS OF THRILLS OF LAUGHTER (U).
MINORS' MATINEE EVERY SATURDAY MORNING
Doors open 9.30 Commence 10.00 a.m.
ABC

Explore Britain by Train
SPECIAL TRIPS AT SPECIAL PRICES
Seaside Excursion
SUNDAY, 5th AUGUST
SKEGNESS £1.10
(Children 55p)
Alfreton depart 10.30 Return at 19.15
Book now to avoid disappointment
Why not take a TWOSOME ticket from Alfreton to
LEICESTER £1.10
NOTTINGHAM 70p
SHEFFIELD 70p
LONDON £3.65
Available for 2 passengers (either 2 Adults or 1 Adult and 1 child) travelling together in both directions.
Outward by any train after 09.30
Return by any train same day
All fares and facilities are subject to alteration or cancellation
For full details of these and many other travel bargains and availability of tickets, ask at your principal station or rail travel agent.
British Rail

New Year's Eve at Chesterfield Transport Social Club

Popular club and cabaret turns Bobby Knutt (left) and Tony Whyte (second from right)

The seventies saw the arrival of Kentucky Fried Chicken in the era

The wonder of Woolies

Outside Castleton's Blue John Cavern

SUSAN CHOSEN AS 'COAL QUEEN'

The new "Queen", Miss Susan Lee, with runners-up Miss Glenys Parker (left) and Mrs. Nita Crew.

LANGWITH Colliery's Coal Queen for [illegible], chosen at a dance at Langwith Welfare Institute on Tuesday, is Miss Susan Sara Lee, of [illegible] Terrace, Langwith.

BUXTON 'POP' FESTIVAL
AT BOOTH FARM, NR. BUXTON, DERBYSHIRE
STOP PRESS: Wizzard; Nazareth appearances now confirmed. Contractural problems over billing now overcome.
ONE ONLY SPECIAL U.K. APPEARANCE
CHUCK BERRY
WIZZARD
WITH SPECIAL GUESTS
CANNED HEAT
GROUNDHOGS
NAZARETH
MEDICINE HEAD
EDGAR BROUGHTON
Plus groups to be announced
D.J. John Peel
Next Weekend—SATURDAY, JULY 21
11.30 a.m. till midnight approx.
ADVANCE TICKETS £2.00 (£2.50 ON DAY)

Dazzled by the fireworks on offer

Radio Hallam's Roger Moffat interviews a Womble

Chesterfield Town Hall

RIVAL BRIGHT LIGHTS FOR SPECIAL OCCASIONS

The Fiesta, biggest nightclub in Europe

Though the bright lights of Chesterfield were entertainment enough for many; nearby Sheffield (and sometimes Nottingham) definitely had more than its fair share of attractions for people.

Its glitzy Fiesta club - being double the size of the Aquarius - pulled in some of the biggest stars on the planet to entertain the masses; Beach Boys, Jackson Five, Stevie Wonder, Shirley Bassey - they all did their weekly residencies in Steel City.

The 1,000+ capacity auditorium was a sight to behold and landing a job as a Fiesta Fawn - the glamorous waitresses - was a dream come true to many females of the era.

Restaurant, disco, its own house band and the most palatial dressing rooms this side of Vegas. All went swimmingly until the staff went on strike in 1976 and the venue ended up being sold.

Though it soldiered on until 1980, things were never quite the same again.

Nowhere got quite as rowdy as the nearby Hofbrauhaus. The venue that welcomed dancing on the tables, beer glasses the size of buckets and oompah band.

Coach parties would regularly arrive from Chesterfield and this was one of the places to celebrate birthdays and other notable milestones.

Fanny's at Owler Bar was a big pull; meanwhile the rockers would decamp to the Wapentake or, earlier in the era, the Buccaneer Bars that used to sit under the Grand Hotel on Leopold Street.

The Limit welcomed the punks when it opened in 1978 and other venues that struck a chord with Chesterfield included

the Crazy Daizy, Penny Farthing, Josephines and Scamps.

And if we weren't partying we were shopping for the clobber that we'd wear for the night out.

Sheffield was home to towering retailers of the era like Cockaynes, Pauldens, Redgates, Walsh's, Sexy Rexy and scores of other household names.

Bowie changed everything

Nigel Lockwood: "Bowie was the instigator of a lot of music and fashion trends that influenced everything else in the era.

"Seeing David Bowie at the Top Rank on September 6, 1972, was the thing that changed everything for me - that and seeing him perform 'Star Man' on Top of the Pops.

"What that did for a lot of other people is made them form bands.

"The only merchandise on sale were two posters - I've still got them both. That was the first rock gig I went to. The second was The Faces at Sheffield City Hall in December 1972. They came on at 10pm and Rod Stewart was kicking footballs out into the audience.

"The other major gig that really affected me was Mick Ronson at Sheffield City Hall in April 1974 and after that we all went back to the Hallam Towers Hotel to see him.

"Then Roxy Music had more of an influence. I also saw Lou Reed do one of his rare solo shows at Sheffield City Hall. Brian Eno and Status Quo who were brilliant at the time. Sparks, Elton John, Mott The Hoople and Cockney Rebel, who I loved.

"Then came pub rock bands like Doctor Feelgood and the Kursaal Flyers in 1975 that I saw at the Black Swan - they kind of set the genre for what influenced the punk bands in the year after."

The opening of the Fiesta in August 1970

Only T-Rex had a issue with Club Fiesta

Christine Ward (nee Milner) started at the Fiesta when it opened in 1970.

She was the venue's assistant manager and has fond memories of the place.

She said: "The Shadows played the first night at the Fiesta following its official opening by the Mayor.

"It went well at first and then things drifted a bit. It was landing the Four Tops that did it - they could have done a month. They sold the place out and the atmosphere was unbelievable. That's what the Fiesta needed - top artists.

"When Stevie Wonder came we had to bring in extra doormen to stand around the stage to ensure nobody rushed it. By the end of it even the doormen were stood on the tables dancing! It was the most electric night.

"It was the same with the Beach Boys. I thought they were never going to be able to reproduce what they produced on record, but they did.

"The Fiesta was the place to come.

"Acts would probably do a week with us and then go home - they wouldn't do a tour as such. "They'd also do a regular summer season and sometimes pantomime."

But not everyone liked the idea of performing at the cabaret-style of the Fiesta.

T-Rex, who were at the height of their fame when they were booked to play, definitely didn't.

Christine Ward said: "Everything always went wrong when I was on duty on my own. For one night only we'd got T-Rex. I arrived about 6 o'clock in the evening and at 7.30pm their manager came to me and said 'they're not going on'. It was a sell-out and they were due on at 9pm. They decided it wasn't their type of venue.

"I rang comedian Jack Diamond who I knew was in Sheffield and I said: 'Jack, you're going to have to do me the biggest favour you'll ever do me - the main act's not going on and I need you to come and do it for me'. I didn't dare tell him who it was that was refusing to go on.

"As he came in he saw T-Rex. He went to the dressing room and was violently sick and wouldn't go on. I said: 'You've got to do it - this is your big chance and we can get a lot of publicity out of it'.

"Jack was introduced and someone shouted 'Ride a White Swan'. And he said: 'You ride what you want dear and I'll ride what I want'. "

Jack won plaudits for his performance under pretty difficult circumstances.

The Penny Farthing

Memories of Hofbrauhaus

Eileen Marriott: "Oompah band and standing on the tables and drinking litre steins of German beer - whether you liked it or not. (I did, & still do)."
Linda Jean Stevens: "It was a raucous night out, that's for sure!"
Jane Kirk: "Went there often. Took a double-decker bus full for my 19th Birthday and got asked out by this lad. 37yrs later and we are still going strong. Ended back at Jingles afterwards. I remember the ladies toilets always getting swamped by the end of the night."
Mick Spracklen: "I remember a few Robinsons coach trips there.
Oompah band and dancing on the tables with a Stein in each hand was mandatory. We used to go to the Jingles regularly too. My mate used to pay wages down at TI on a Thursday night and he'd have to leg it back up town so that we could get in before 9.30pm with our free tickets."
Pat Bennett: "Worked there 3 nights a week in 1974/75. Used to carry 5 steins in each hand. Sure built ones muscles up!"
Lynn Jones: "It was fab - went on so many 21st birthdays there! Ein Prosit ..."
Anne Marie Oakley: "Went there regularly when it was anyone's birthday, then sometimes into Scamps nightclub next door after if not too drunk. lol xx."
Phil Clayton: "I do remember being in there one night with 'little' Dennis Hackett. We were talking (if that's the word) to Alan Kilby the deaf & dumb wrestler. He was a bouncer at Eve & Acca I think."

Publicity shot for the opening of the Hofbrauhaus

The resident ompaah band of the Hofbrauhaus

The Hofbrauhaus entrance on Eyre Street

ELVIS SAYS 'NO' TO BRITAIN, BUT—

SHEFFIELD FIESTA

The newspaper of Europe's top night spot No.6

WILL HE ACCEPT OUR INVITATION?

SPECIAL EDITION

ELVIS FOR THE FIESTA?

An open letter to the king of pop

From Keith & Jim Lipthorpe

The background—

THE New Musical Express, one of the world's leading show business newspapers, which is distributed throughout the United States as well as Britain, stated in their main front page article of September 16th:

"After years of speculation Elvis Presley and Colonel Tom Parker have finally said NO to a British tour of concerts. Reason given is that no suitable British venue exists at the present time.

In talks with British fan club organiser Todd Slaughter, the Colonel has ruled out what he calls "ball parks" — an apparent reference to Wembley — and instead wants a supper club showcase for Elvis with seating for upwards of 1,000 diners.

"This would be similar to the Las Vegas International (Now Hilton) featured in the Elvis film 'That's The Way It Is', but no such nightspot exists in this country at the present time.

According to Todd Slaughter the Colonel believes that "no singer can do justice to himself in a ball park". Elvis said he would appear if the right venue existed."

Immediately following this article—which was highlighted by a number of newspapers—the Fiesta sent a strong protest to the N.M.E. which resulted in an article headlined "Sheffield challenge to Presley rebuff".

Now, after much deliberation, Keith and Jim Lipthorpe, the Fiesta's owners, have sent an open letter addressed personally to Presley.

PLEASE TURN TO BACK PAGE

Memories of the Fiesta

Eileen Marriott: "I remember going there in red hot pants with bib and braces. Thought I looked the bee's knees till I got there - guess what all the waitresses were wearing???"

Jane Kirk: "Saw Jimmy Ruffin there and the Three Degrees. My sister had her Hen Night there."

Jayne Burgess: "I'm pretty sure my Mum and Dad went to see Guys and Dolls there, they went regularly on a weekend... Might have to raid my parents' old photo albums lol."

Richard Sandy: "The Fiesta was absolutely awesome. We'd be there every single weekend. It was one of the plushest venues I've ever been to, anywhere in the world. Nothing could match it at that time. The nearby Cavendish couldn't touch it. "Club Fiesta persuaded the biggest American acts in the world to perform up close and personal with Sheffield: Stevie Wonder, Four Tops, The Beach Boys and Jackson 5 complete with Michael Jackson were just a few of the household names to make the trip."

Dancing the night away at the Fiesta

The Buccaneer - rock'n'roll central

Buccaneer landlady Olga Marshall

There was rarely a quiet night at the Hofbrauhaus

Silver Jubilee street parties were played out across the town in 1977

CHAPTER TEN

THREE TV CHANNELS WAS ENTERTAINMENT APLENTY

Courtesy of Chesterfield Photographic Society and www.picturethepast.org.uk

There were no PCs, laptops, tablets, Xboxes or smart phones in the 1970s. There was also far less obesity. Connection? You betcha.

The outdoor life for kids was a way of life. It was all a far cry from the paranoia of 21st century society where people feel more at home arguing on Facebook rather than exchanging pleasantries over the garden fence.

There was also less chance of staying glued to the TV; there were only three channels, no breakfast TV and all presenters were tucked up in bed by midnight.

The quality and longevity of many of the TV shows have deservedly outlasted the confines of the era - in fact many have helped define it.

'Are You Being Served', which first hit the airwaves in 1972, has enjoyed a life far beyond the 1970s for the fictional Grace Brothers clothing store.

The decade belonged to Morecambe & Wise whose weekend show seemed to dominate every Saturday night - before Match of the Day at any rate.

Saturday morning kids TV was never the same again after the rise of Tiswas (which was actually short for the rather the bizarre sounding, 'Today is Saturday, Watch and Smile') which ran amok from 1974 onwards.

Daytime TV was kept in check by the soothing tones of Derek Batey and his 'Mr & Mrs' quiz show.

No sitcom left quite the legacy as 'Love Thy Neighbour' which ran for seven series from 1972 until 1976.

The plot was based around a suburban white working class couple who unwittingly found themselves living next door to a black couple. The sitcom was huge.

'Love Thy Neighbour' exemplified an issue that was happening up and down the country at the time; Britain coming to terms with recently arrived population of black immigrants.

The views of the white male character (Eddie Booth, played by Jack Smethurst) were presented in such a way as to make him appear stupid and bigoted, and were contrasted with the more tolerant attitude of his wife.

His use of terms such as 'nig-nog' to refer to his black neighbour, despite being intended as ironic by the scriptwriters, attracted considerable criticism from viewers. The male black character was, in contrast educated and sophisticated, although stubborn and also capable of racism using the terms 'honky', 'snowflake', 'paleface' or 'big white chief' to describe his white neighbour.

These days, if the series is repeated, it normally comes with a content warning beforehand...

There's no doubt the 1970s were the masters of the sitcom; 'The Good Life', 'Fawlty Towers', 'Some Mothers Do 'Ave 'Em', 'Rising Damp' and 'Whatever Happened To The Likely Lads' to give a few examples.

Some just ran and ran - for the duration of the era in some cases.

There wasn't another era like it. The eighties went left of centre with alternative comedy like 'The Young Ones'; there was only really one show, 'Only Fools and Horses', that really came close to the family sitcoms that ruled the 1970s.

It's no surprise that the era is regularly referred to as the golden age of television.

There was no prize better than being the first one in the house to get your hands on the bumper Christmas TV Times or Radio Times.

You were the first one to circle the programmes you were going to watch in this festive bonanza.

In an age before video recorders the Yuletide period was a televisual feast like nothing else on earth.

The Royal Hospital which served the town in the era.

Staveley High Street

The future Pomegranate Theatre

The Portland - an essential stop off on many a '70s pub crawl

The long gone Horns Hotel (right)

Courtesy of Chesterfield Photographic Society and www.picturethepast.org.uk

Retiring to a smaller place

Mr. and Mrs. George Allen pictured outside the Town Hall which has been their home and their work.

GEORGE ALLEN lost his job, and his home, last weekend — but he's not complaining . . .

For 65-year-old George retired from his post as steward at Chesterfield Town Hall — and had to move out of his top-floor flat at the Town Hall as well.

Now, after 15 years of living literally on top of his their retirement home at Loundsley Green.

George's stewardship ended on a right royal note — for he was formally presented to the Queen and the Duke of Edinburgh during the Royal visit to Chesterfield in July.

Before taking up his Town Hall post in 1962, Mr. Allen was employed by the Chesterfield Co-operative Society, including a spell as grocery manager.

Mr. and Mrs. Allen have

'ST. TRINIANS' GIRLS AT DRONFIELD GALA

Trinians was the theme of the Millthorpe Metals float and the girls in our picture ered into the spirit of the thing with gusto at the Dronfield Gala on Saturday.

Family occasions were always worth getting dressed up for

Nearby Matlock

Matlock cable cars sponsored by Skol

Hair Flair of West Bars

Inside Hair Flair on West Bars

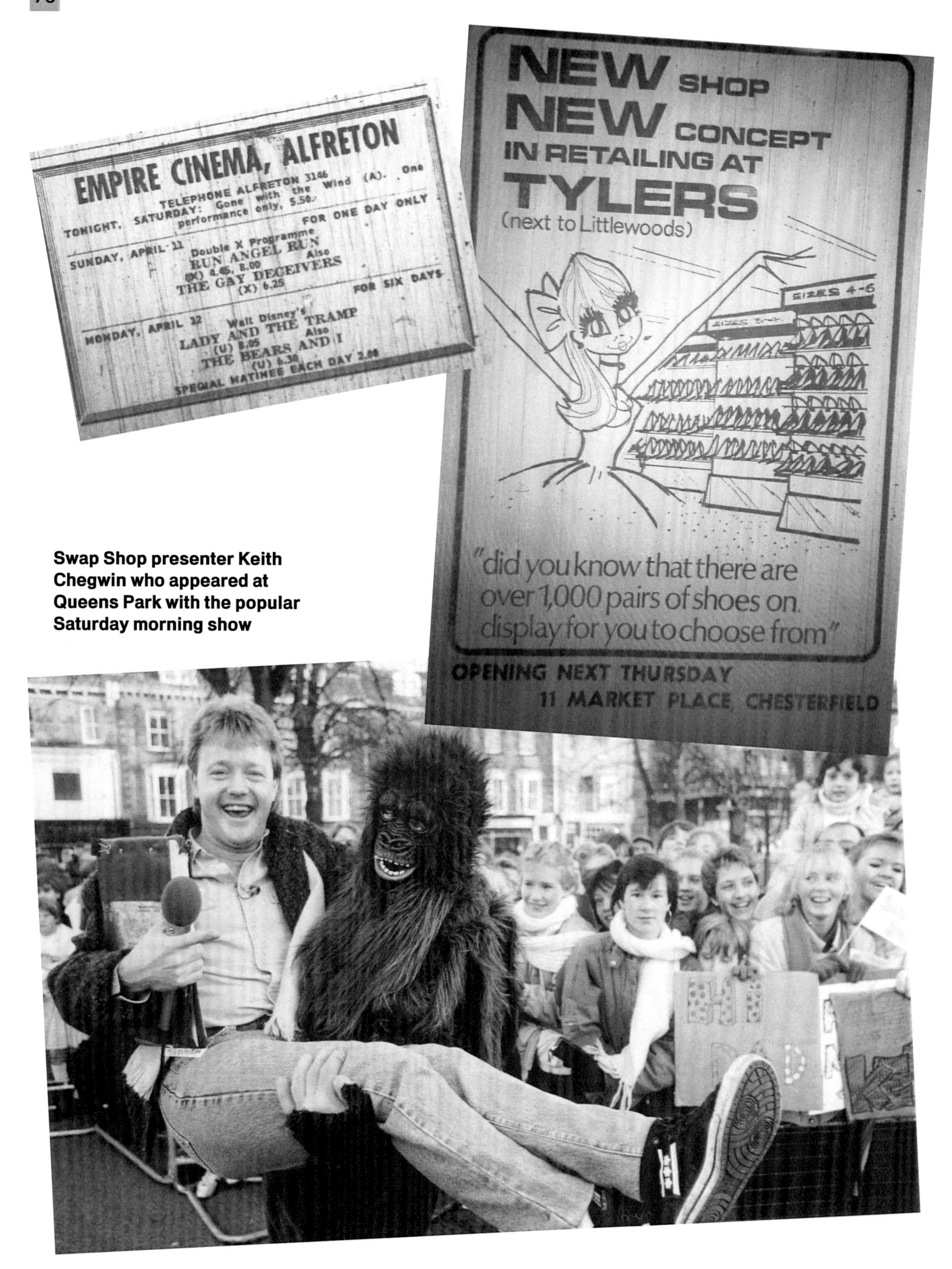

Swap Shop presenter Keith Chegwin who appeared at Queens Park with the popular Saturday morning show

Chesterfield's UK club of the year

No venue finished the 1970s in quite such match fit fashion as the Aquarius.

The venue was voted the top nightclub in the entire country by Club Mirror and won their prestigious 'Club of the Year Award' in 1979.

Plaudits didn't come any higher. The venue had come a long way since it first opened to the public on November 9th, 1972.

The Spanish themed venue with a total capacity of 1,600 had become a cornerstone of after dark Chesterfield.

Tommy Tuft was the popular compère at the venue that was operating seven nights a week.

Catering at the club got a particular mention as part of the celebrations. Notable dishes included fillet steak au poivre; grilled fillet garni; grilled rainbow trout meuniere and, of course, the ever popular basket meals.

AQUARIUS

PRESENTATION NIGHT OF

CLUB MIRROR

CLUB OF THE YEAR AWARD

TUESDAY, 6th MARCH, 1979

SOUVENIR PROGRAMME

Proceeds in Aid of the National Spastics Society

John Williamson, general manager and director

Aquarius security

Administration staff

Annual staff party

See which members of staff you can remember from the Aquarius department heads that helped them win the award:

The author

Neil Anderson

Neil Anderson first launched the 'Dirty Stop Out's Guide(TM)' as part of a PR campaign in the mid-1990s to help regenerate Sheffield's nightlife. Since then he has written a whole retro series for the city.

Neil Anderson grew up in Chesterfield in the 1970s and 1980s, road tested the town pretty well and is still a regular visitor.

He has written on nightlife and entertainment for titles spanning The Independent to The Big Issue and was a Sheffield Telegraph columnist for 12 years.

In 2013 he wrote local best seller, the 'Dirty Stop Out's Guide to 1980s Chesterfield'.

By day he runs Neil Anderson Media - a public relations company.

Acknowledgements

Thanks to: Sharon Bull, Andy Mott, Stuart Smith, Bernie Clifton, Michele Quinn, Stephanie Wonder Trousers, Carl Flint, Martin Edwards, Maria Davison, Helen Watson-Jones, Les Oakley, Linda Biggs, Lynn Jones, Jane Kirk, Dave Stone, John Williamson, Dave Plumb, Helen Plumb, Kate Ogilby, Dave Allen, Julie Batty, Jane Salt, Nancy Fielder, Graeme Huston, Julia Rodgerson, Caroline Gowing, Keith Brisland, Pete Hill, Olga Marshall, Elaine Hall, Chesterfield Local Studies Library, Derrick Scattergood, Nick Tomlinson, Jacqueline Hanson, Les Oakley, Terry Knowles and Linda Jean Stevens.

All round inspiration: Lindsay McLaren.

Proofing: Peter Eales.

Balancing the books: Ian Cheetham.

Layout: Karen Davies.

Dedicated to Lowri, Ewan and Dylan Anderson.

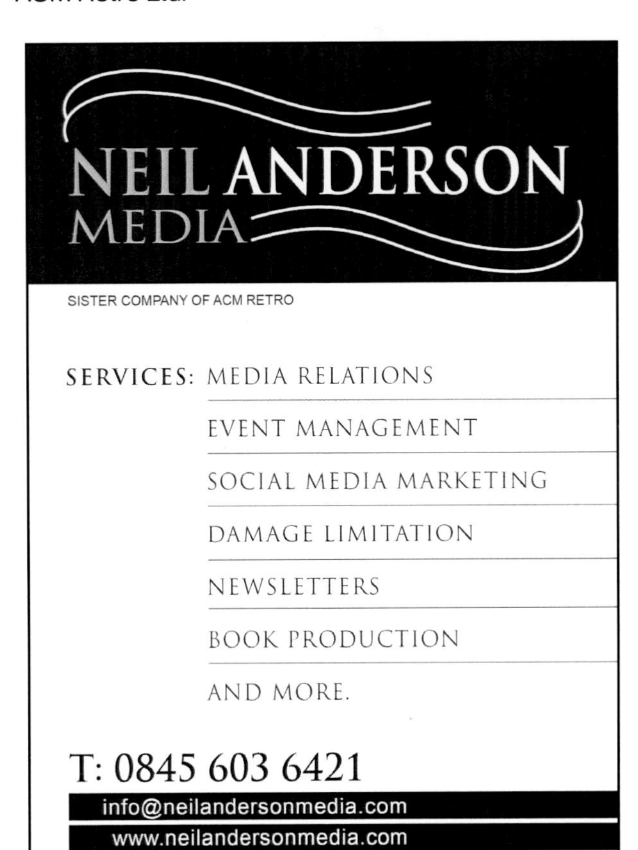

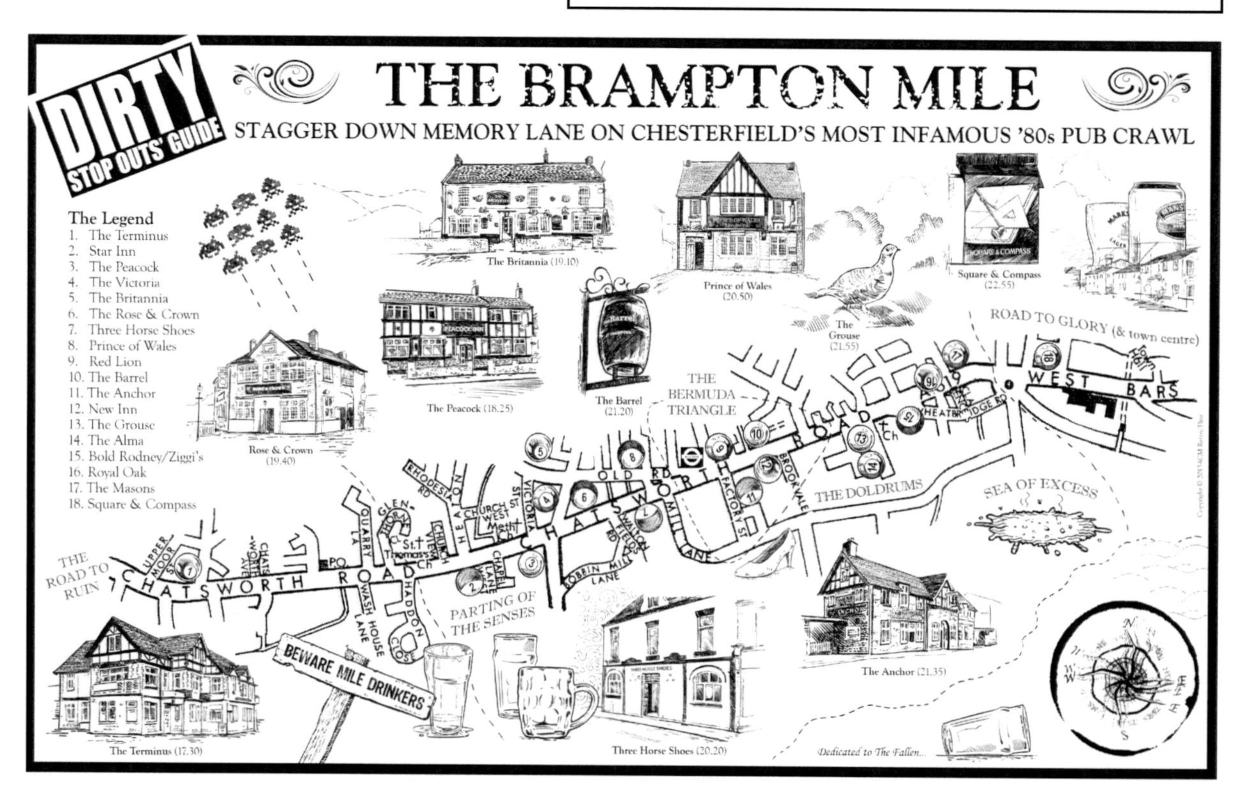

Commemorative tea towel

www.picturethepast.org.uk

Picturing the Past...

In the past, anyone wanting to view the collections of hundreds of thousands of old images in the libraries and museums of Derbyshire or Nottinghamshire would have had to travel many miles to try and track down the ones they were interested in. This proved to be frustrating and time-consuming for researchers, a barrier to anyone from further afield and damaging to the more fragile images due to all the handling. The collections include photographs, slides, negatives, glass plates, postcards and engravings recalling the history of our local communities over the past hundred years and more.

Thankfully, staff in four local authorities got their heads together to solve the problem, and the idea of conserving the images using digitisation, while at the same time giving people all over the world access to the digitised versions, was conceived. With initial funding from the Heritage Lottery at the beginning of 2002, the four partner authorities, Derbyshire and Nottinghamshire County Councils and the City Councils of Derby and Nottingham set up the project.

Local studies staff in the libraries and museums started collating images and information ready for inclusion in the project and sent out thousands of letters requesting copyright clearance from the original photographers or their relatives. Nick Tomlinson was appointed as project manager to lead a team of experienced professionals inputting the information into a custom-built database and carefully digitising the images.

The Picture the Past website (www.picturethepast.org.uk) was launched in June 2003 and by the beginning of 2013 over 100,000 pictures had been added. It now attracts well over 15,000 visitors each month from all over the world.

The site is updated on a regular basis and actually gives the user the ability to 'correct' existing information or add more information to those pictures with scant details.

Designed to be as easy to use as possible, the website includes a simple keyword search facility as well as more comprehensive search mechanisms for users looking for images with a particular theme or by a specific photographer. Visitors can print out low resolution copies for their own personal use or study purposes, but for those users wanting to own a top-quality photographic copy the website includes an online ordering service with all the income raised from this service going back into the conservation and preservation of more original pictures.

This book includes just a handful of the images that appear on the website and it is very much hoped that you will go on to enjoy some of the other pictures online.

The website can be viewed at www.picturethepast.org.uk

Courtesy of Derbyshire Local Studies Library and www.picturethepast.org.uk

Looking towards the bus station